CUSTOM

MANIFESTO

HOW TO GET CLIENTS TO STAY LONGER, FEEL HAPPY AND ACHIEVE BETTER RESULTS

JAY GONCALVES

BEN MCLELLAN

ISBN: 9798365494824

Imprint: Independently published.

CONTENTS

Contents

Contents

INTRODUCTION

"It's quite a good ethos for life: go into the unknown with truth, commitment, and openness, and mostly you'll be okay."

Alan Cumming

Here we are, the three of us, with a candle burning in the background, chill music, and reading a new book about how to make your service excellent. All of us want a great business that can scale to hundreds of happy customers, that gets close to no drop-offs, and to have a team that's empowered and not burnt out.

Or maybe you bought this book in a time of stress because everything is burning, and you feel like your business is a leaky bucket...

Everything is fine. Nothing to be concerned about

If it's the latter, we've all been there. A business owner rarely has the mental space or energy to be preventative and fix things before they break.

The negativity bias gets us to pay much more attention to things going wrong than things going great. And Ben and I created this book with that in mind. If you're feeling like there is much more to be done in how you serve your clients, we're going to make it simple, easy, and efficient by showing you how to use this book as your roadmap.

For a long time, marketers have been making bolder and bolder promises, specifically in the online space. We started with promises of building a six-figure business (expert or agency). Then everyone was promising a seven-figure business, and nowadays, they promise you multiple seven figures without even working.

Marketers believe you need more and more clients to get what you want from life. You might have fallen prey to that, pumping more money into ads, hiring appointment setters, and having a massive sales team.

But going through that process, you realize how acquisition gets more expensive, your business gets more complex, you're living in the middle of chaos, and you can barely sleep.

This leads to underappreciated value; you're so focused on delivering more and more that you miss the delivery of a remarkable experience that gives your clients enjoyment, which will make them appreciate your efforts, refer more people and stay with you longer.

This makes you feel out of integrity and not even close to your goal: Freedom.

Freedom of time, of headaches, and the rollercoaster of uncertainty.

Before we keep going, who are we, and why should you care about what we have to share with you?

Meet Jay and Ben

My name is João Gonçalves (Jay for short), and you won't meet someone as focused as I am. I'll go above and beyond to meet my client's expectations and deliver on Ethical Scaling's mission. I'll be the one writing most of the book in the first person, so whenever you read "I," it's Jay, unless I explicitly say that Ben is the one sharing his wisdom.

Born and raised in Portugal, I always had this entrepreneurial dream of making a difference and always felt I had something unique to offer. Exploring some of the opportunities life gave me, today I'm here with you, writing in my second language (English).

The catalyst for my initial business endeavors was a different type of scale. A scale that told me I needed to lose 100 pounds or my life would be at risk.

I realized it would require more than just eating well and exercising to achieve this goal. This challenge required me to understand human behavior and how to form a winning & repeatable process.

Through behavioral change protocols, I developed my own business to deliver high-quality health services to a few thousand people. That business helped me develop systems and strategies to provide high-quality coaching to more than 150 active clients at a time. It wasn't long before I understood how I could help your business do the same.

And then I met Ben McLellan. I'll let him share his background .

A rift was forming... My life was divided between becoming a successful business owner and a father that keeps his family together. There was always a nagging feeling in the back of my mind about starting my own business.

I got my start in the online space after selling my yoga and fitness studio. The opening of a new phase led me to become a part of Traffic and Funnels' ClientKit program. I worked my way onto the team that supported about 250 clients simultaneously.

I was promoted to Client Success Director after 6 months. Over 24 months, I oversaw the journey of more than a thousand clients and a team of seven coaches. I also saw TF go from a multi-seven figure to an eight-figure consulting company.

When discussing a move to Nashville, where the TF headquarters was, my wife had had enough, "You're not even here when you're here. What is going on?"

As soon as I realized I was allowing my job to destroy my marriage and family, I decided to take my destiny into my own hands.

I gave my notice to leave and ended up joining another company, but left that new company a few months later as I felt out of alignment.

I played too small, trying to support other people's missions and visions. It was time to unleash my own.

Hence, the start of Ethical Scaling.

Jay and I came up with Ethical Scaling and our Consulting Service, The Raving Fan Formula, and the rest is history.

At its core, Ethical Scaling is about running your business in line with your values. This principle is the foundation of how we guide business owners to build a profitable, sustainable, and fulfilling company.

We help multi 6, 7, and 8-figure online service-based businesses take world-class care of their clients to increase profitability, maintain an outstanding reputation, and operate with integrity.

You can find more information here: ethicalscaling.com

Scan me for more information

The epiphany

Why haven't business owners made customer success a priority before?

The answer is simple: customer success is preventative, and humans are reactive by default. People rarely go to the gym to prevent disease. They sign up to treat sickness. Almost no one searches for help to deliver the best customer experience to their clients; they search for how to get more clients.

Everyone thinks about how to prevent churn instead of seeing customer success as the most profitable part of their business. It's an opportunity to generate even more revenue while serving clients well.

I don't judge it. It's how humans are wired. Thinking upstream is unnatural for most of us. But take a moment to think about your clients: what is it really like for them using your service?

Is there any "sickness" that you should be addressing in your customer experience? If it was any other symptom in your life, would you ignore it or get it treated quickly and easily with guidance and support?

After consulting with over a hundred businesses and being business owners ourselves for more than ten years, we see the same problems everywhere.

Whenever we see a great business owner dealing with most of their clients dropping off, a lot of clients not crossing the finish line, struggling to keep clients for longer than six months, and a team that's in constant burn out... We know it's time for an intervention.

After coaching thousands of people and running several businesses ourselves, we've been lucky enough to observe patterns and trends about what is working, what is not, and where things are going.

Some of the most exciting projects we have seen follow a typical S-curve growth pattern like the one depicted below:

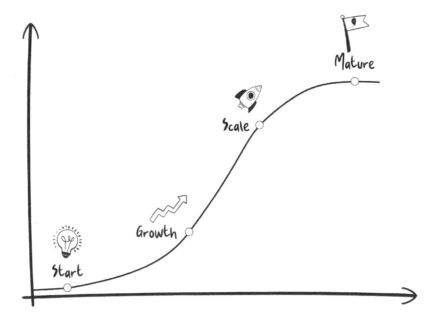

Think about the Telephone by Alexander Bell, Zappos, or even Apple. These are examples of S-curve business ideas.

Most of the Tech companies that were or are a great success tend to follow this S-curve, Moore's law is one of the key factors that causes it.

Moore's law is a term used to refer to the observation made by Gordon Moore in 1965 that the number of transistors in a dense integrated circuit (IC) doubles about every two years.

Look at our industry, the high ticket industry might not have a lot of transistors, but the number of scammers overpromising has more than doubled every two years. That's scary.

Moore's Law was adapted to this industry by Alen Sultanic. He calls it the *Morons Law*.

Jokes aside, there is a lot to be learned from the best and fastest-growing companies in the world.

You'll see things differently when you realize that we're all living in an exponential age where things change at a speed we can barely comprehend. As a result, the best companies in the world can deliver more at lower costs.

How can we apply this to service-based businesses online or maybe even brick-and-mortar businesses?

This hasn't been appropriately implemented from what we've witnessed. Because if it was, you would be living your dream: working as many hours as you'd like, you'd have an efficient, happy and engaged team, and your business would be super profitable without you being concerned every month about your cashflow or feeling like your business keeps hitting the ceiling.

Equipped with the information you have now, you can understand where the service-based business space will be moving in a short time. The ones that crack the code will have a long-lasting business and finally have the certainty of a life of freedom.

And most of what you'll see in this book is a typical conversation we have with growing companies that onboard 20-30 clients a month. The faster the company grows, the more they feel the need for proper Account Manager or Coaches training.

Most owners don't feel like being in the trenches coaching their team on the nitty-gritty; they have other important things to do. We get it.

At the same time, you will be surprised when you see your team underperforming, very little retention in your business, and burnout everywhere. Just like when you hired an agency to run your ads, or a remote closer company to place one or more closers, it might be time to get someone to go in the trenches and train your team to optimize your Fulfillment Funnel. It could be us, or it could be an integrator of yours after reading this book. But it must get done.

This will help create remarkable experiences and get more clients to cross the finish line while keeping them ecstatic about renewing.

We will help you embody three words that lead to a highly profitable and sustainable business: Relationships at Scale.

Simple right? Yeah, I know, easier said than done, and thus why we're here.

For the past two years, we've been doing this with our Consulting experience, the Raving Fan Formula, where we've helped more than a hundred businesses install a Fulfillment Funnel™.

I'd love to go over all the details and pillars of the Raving Fan Formula with you today, but I'll save that for another time. Another book, who knows?

Here is a very high-level view of what we do with the Raving Fan Formula:

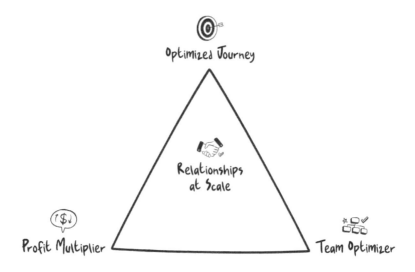

The three pillars of the Raving Fan Formula are:

- **Optimized Journey**: this pillar focuses on building a smooth journey, typically for your entry offer, which most people buy when they start working with you. This allows you to deliver a great experience to your clients and <u>eliminate drop-offs and refunds.</u>

- **Profit Multiplier**: this pillar focuses on creating an offer suite, which means expanding the options for clients to work with you for longer. It could mean extending the Journey they started or having them invest in an entirely new backend offer that allows them to ascend and fly higher. The goal is to build a sequence between offers that makes them more valuable connected than if they were experienced separately. <u>And when this is dialed in, your</u>

<u>clients will stay 4x longer.</u>

- **Team Optimize**r: This pillar focuses on your team being able to drive your voice and mission forward, ensuring they understand what the business wants as a whole, how to create those meaningful relationships with clients, and performing at a high level <u>without them burning out.</u>

Those are the three pillars we go through when working with our Consulting clients, and depending on what they need, we might work on one pillar or the three of them. It's always catered to the client.

Irrespective of how many pillars we work on, the main goal of the three is to create an opportunity for great relationships with clients and to become client-centric.

We know that giving you an actionable framework that can be implemented after a short read will bring you all the things you need to embrace this new evolution of how to do business.

You'll be able to increase your Client Lifetime Value, accommodate higher acquisition costs, increase profitability and make competition irrelevant.

And how will you do that? That's what you'll find in the *Customer Success Manifesto*.

This book's goal is to bring as much attention to the fulfillment of your service as you do to marketing and sales. Clients are tired of buying, entering the Pain Funnel, where they can't get what they want, and feeling frustrated, overwhelmed, and deceived.

During your acquisition process, you do calls, send emails, SMS, retargeting campaigns, and probably even have community groups until prospects become clients. Then your focus changes, and you start focusing on cost savings around the customer success department and THAT is killing your business.

Trying to convince customers not to ask for support, making interactions as brief as possible, and always trying to minimize the cost of delivery will put you out of business.

This book will be contrarian, and I hope you'll have an open mind to go through it, as I know you're data-driven, you understand science, and you don't want to conform to what everyone is doing without understanding it.

Before we go into the tactical stuff we love and that you want, we'll give you a guide on how to best use this book in the next chapter.

We want to close this introduction by saying that your business is more than just a source of income. It reflects your core values and who you are as a person.

It's easy to think we have to be someone other than who we are to hit 'bigger' goals. But, we have repeatedly found that the key to experiencing what you truly want is staying true to who you are.

I. YOUR BOOK GUIDE

"We must tell our customers how great their life can look if they buy our products and services."

Donald Miller

How the book is structured

This book will be divided into several chapters:

1. The Book Guide will help you navigate through the book and find which sections might be used daily as a guide to working with clients.

2. Foundations will go through the misconceptions we're seeing in the marketplace that keep business owners spinning their wheels without getting a feeling of freedom.

3. The Fulfillment Continuum explains what clients will be paying attention to, how to get them to show up, and how

you want them to benefit from the offer they purchased.

4. Archetypes will describe different clients and communication styles, which will connect all the book concepts in a way that makes sense for the client success team.

5. The Application goes into detail about what will give you the best bang for your buck while exploring examples of how to get these frameworks implemented immediately.

6. A Bonus section with the most relevant actions and examples you can implement after finishing the book.

How to extract the most out of it

We highly recommend this process to get the most out of this book:

- Please go through the whole book to understand all the concepts and technical jargon and to understand the main ideas.

- After absorbing the Foundations chapter, analyze your business from a foundational point of view.

- Ask your team to go through the Fulfillment Continuum chapter and identify areas of opportunity to make the process simpler for clients.

- Get your team to use the Archetypes daily when working with clients, and have the book with them as a playbook; this will release a lot of the micromanaging needed from you.

- After a couple of weeks, go through the Application chapter again, read the Bonus Section again, and create a 90-day plan on what could be optimized to increase Client Lifetime Value (LTV).

Gift your customer success team members a copy of the book, go through the clinics with them, and join our community to gather feedback. You can search for the Facebook Group: Ethical Scaling.

Scan me to join our community

I don't want this book to sound like a pitch because nobody loves a pitch fest. But from a place of service and empathy, if you ever feel like we can work with you to implement this, or you would like us to train your team 1:1, make sure to reach out to us. You can find more information on our website ethicalscaling.com.

Scan me for more information

Before we move on: R&D for business innovation

I want to share a couple of concepts that can help you use all the ideas in this book without feeling overwhelmed or feeling like you need to do it all yourself.

To focus on all the concepts, you need to find a tradeoff between Exploit and Explore:

- Exploit what you know.

- Explore what you don't know.

Your business might be over-optimized for the past and the data you have, making your system overly rigid and not allowing you to find the unknown. Some of that unknown could be in this book.

If you can find someone on your team who loves to be an integrator, that can read the book alongside you, give them a little time and permission to explore; you will get

outcomes you didn´t think possible. Effective delegation is a big part of being a great leader.

Introducing the Implementation Clinics

In this book, you'll find several clinics where we give examples that show how to implement the concepts in real life so that you can brainstorm with your team on how to do it.

II. FOUNDATIONS

180°

Before we go and start laying out the quick start and how to get the most out of this book, let me tell you why this book is built the way it is. I promise to keep it short, but I want to contextualize it.

Not long ago, I was a Systems Engineer. And I crushed it, not only because my brain is wired to think in systems but because there was a secret sauce I had that almost no one else did.

This secret sauce helped me go from being hired and subsequently dumped to becoming one of the most valuable assets for this company and managing the Qatar Olympic Games project with a Work Package of 100M+ and a Team of 5.

So what happened? What was the secret sauce?

I was great at communicating with our clients and all the stakeholders. I also found that I was great at managing accounts and having high-stakes conversations. I could convey the truth but adapt my communication style to the person I was talking to. I nailed the Archetypal approach, and you'll understand later in the book what that means.

This skill was pivotal when my business skyrocketed from a couple of clients to almost two hundred. I could manage the Relationships at Scale.

On the other hand, Ben almost killed himself trying to manage relationships at scale. See, when he was the Client Success Director at Traffic and Funnels, he oversaw the team, but he also led 80 of the 250 clients personally.

He refused to let those clients walk through the program without direction, so he watched over those 80 as if they were his own. And he learned how and when to communicate with them to help them stay clear along their journey.

So, while Ben had the understanding and skill of using archetypes in coaching, he didn't have Jay's system-building skills. And that's one of the reasons we work so well together.

Owning these skills and making them repeatable allows us to create great relationships and retention in our business (90%+).

We've been able to create an amazing client experience that keeps the majority of our clients working with us for 12 months or more. This has led us to high Client Lifetime Value (LTV for short), and we can afford as many clients as we want because retaining clients has made our business profits grow exponentially.

Ben and I have both learned that Fulfillment is not an expense, but a Revenue Generating Department in our business that creates optionality, stability and lots of growth.

When your Fulfillment Funnel is profitable and generates monthly recurring revenue, you can:

- Decide not to take on new clients because you have plenty of them.

- Acquire more clients without eating profits, as you have ample cash generated from current clients.

- You can finally hire a team and remove yourself because the extra money can be used to hire talent.

This was the time when I stopped seeing Acquisition Funnels as the only way to make money. We now had proof of concept with our first solid Fulfillment Funnel™. But what is a Fulfillment Funnel™?

The Fulfillment Funnel™

Now you know that fulfillment can bring you good things like extra profit, cash flow, monthly recurring revenue, and raving fans. Let's go step by step so you can start using a clinical lens to look at your fulfillment and offers.

This will help you create a cohesive story for your business, a story that doesn't contradict itself. The flow should be smooth and enjoyable across marketing, sales, and fulfillment.

After the 100M offer book came to the market, everyone had an epiphany about how critical high LTVs are. We are so thankful that an Influencer like Alex Hormozi took the time to spread the message we've been pushing since 2019.

The focus on high LTV will allow you to accommodate high Ad spend (higher acquisition costs), and it helps to create healthy culture and profit. Win-win.

How can you do it? Can you increase your offer's perceived value? Will it change your business?

The perceived value of the offer is what allows you to:

- Charge Higher Prices

- Give better client experiences

- Hire really good team members and compensate them well

This is possible with a fulfillment funnel, but what is a funnel?

Let's look at your business. Almost any business has this flow for acquisition (or variation):

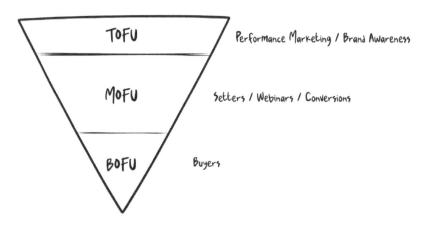

Your acquisition funnel will include at least three big parts. What we call:

- **TOFU:** Top of Funnel

    - This is where you focus on branding, awareness, and getting people to know about you.

    - It can include Lead Magnets, Webinars, Community Groups (Fb, Discord, Telegram, Skool Etc.)

- The goal is to get a cold lead to know you and your offerings.

- This is where you typically focus on Problem Awareness. You understand your perfect client's problem, and make them aware of it.

  - *Example: you've been running ads and struggling to keep your profit margins, and although your revenue is going up, you're not necessarily making more money, you see refunds and drop-offs pile up, and the whole team is burned out.*

- **MOFU**: Middle of Funnel

  - This is where you start nurturing people that have already heard about you.

  - It can include setters that have conversations with your prospects when they join your free community. A webinar that helps them understand their problem and book a call with you, where you focus on converting more people to get closer to you and what you do.

  - This is where you focus on Solution Awareness. Now that they're aware of their problem, what Solution can help them get rid of it?

- *Example: you know running ads and getting more clients won't work by itself to bring you the financial and time freedom you always wanted unless you know how to keep those clients and increase your LTV. Things will eventually break.*

- **BOFU**: Bottom of Funnel

  - This is where you get your prospects to leap and become clients and use your service.

  - This could be achieved with a sales page and checkout process, it could be a sales call for a high-ticket service, or it could even be closing someone using DMs.

  - This is typically where you focus on Product Awareness. Now that they're aware of their Problem and that a Solution exists, you make them aware that you have the Solution built into your product or service.

    - *Example: you've been spending more to get more clients, but profits don't increase, and now you understand that the only way to make that happen is by increasing LTV. Finally, after going through an intro with us, you know that to make that happen, you need to have a system that supports Relationships at Scale. Now you have a formula for extending contracts to at least a year, you can barely see anyone dropping off, and you trust your team to sustain that long term.*

Enough about Marketing, we're not experts on it, but it will help us understand this book's central concept and goal. Let's use the funnel analogy to explain how you can reframe and restructure your fulfillment for profitability.

Little to no business has this in place for their fulfillment, but this is what it should look like:

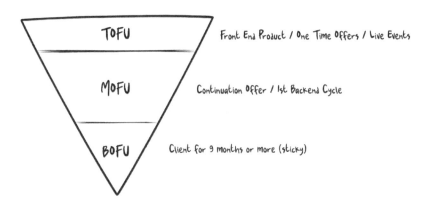

TOFU — Front End Product / One Time Offers / Live Events

MOFU — Continuation Offer / 1st Backend Cycle

BOFU — Client for 9 months or more (sticky)

Your fulfillment funnel will include the same three stages:

- **TOFU**: Top of Funnel

- ○ Usually, your client's first purchase.

- ○ It can include a Front End Product like your flagship program, could be a One-Time Offer, Access to a Mastermind or Community, or even a Live Event.

- ○ This happens when they pay for the first time and assume they want to solve their problem and see your business as a possible guide to solve it.

- **MOFU**: Middle of Funnel

  - ○ This is where you convert people to a second purchase.

  - ○ It can be a repurchase, meaning they will buy more of the same offer if you're running a monthly recurring payment for a community or mastermind. It could be a continuation offer after they go through your Front End Flagship Offer or a Share of Wallet if you sell them a new service that complements or stacks on top of the first one.

- **BOFU**: Bottom of Funnel

  - ○ This is where you work with clients that are considered sticky.

  - ○ This could be achieved after nurturing or working

> with a client for more than nine months, and where
> the level of trust, intimacy, and overall relationship
> reaches the level of them becoming a Raving Fan.

Acquisition funnels and Fulfillment funnels are different, and I want to explain why people are overly-focused on the acquisition and not as much on the fulfillment funnel. They don't understand the overlap, and they (that's you) need to understand how to connect both funnels as one.

This connected funnel is what is called The Bow-Tie Funnel. It's the interconnection between a great acquisition funnel and an excellent fulfillment funnel.

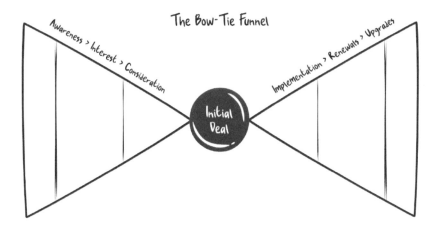

The Fulfillment Funnel™ is the secret sauce we install in our Consulting clients' businesses to help them have a Bow-Tie funnel, and you'll understand why in a second.

When we introduced our Raving Fan Formula, we shared the three pillars:

- **Optimized Journey**: this pillar focuses on building a smooth journey.

- **Profit Multiplier**: this pillar focuses on creating an offer suite.

- **Team Optimizer**: This pillar focuses on your team being able to drive your voice and mission forward.

And those three pillars are the ones that create an effective Fulfillment Funnel™.

The **Optimized Journey** work helps more people go from Top to close to the Middle of the Fulfillment Funnel™.

The **Profit Multiplier** is the offer that brings them from the Middle to the Bottom of the Fulfillment Funnel™.

The **Team Optimizer** trains the team on how to facilitate an amazing client journey that turns clients into raving fans AND how to properly upgrade clients with simple conversations from the Top to the Middle of the Fulfillment Funnel™.

But why is no one else talking about Bow-Tie funnels or about our Fulfillment Funnel™?

Because while marketers are smart, they're still people, so like anyone else, they tend to overinvest in quantifiable things and underinvest in things that are valuable but hard to put a number on. When was the last time you heard about a Bow-Tie Funnel? Probably never, as most people are bought into the idea that acquisition funnels are the key to success. Aren't you just one funnel away?

That's why performance-based campaigns are so popular, and the fulfillment funnel and LTV are not.

It's not that we won't produce results with just a fulfillment funnel, but customer loyalty is slower to measure than conversions, making most anxious business owners focus on acquisition while forgetting the fulfillment funnel. So spending more on the acquisition funnel doesn't make it more effective, but because it's easier to prove quick results, most business owners become obsessed with acquisition.

We need to remember that we never know who our customers will be in advance, we can analyze past data, but it won't necessarily predict the future. It will give us feedback, but if we keep spending on acquisition, we lose a great opportunity. As Ogilvy said:

"You aren't advertising to a standing army; you are advertising to a moving parade."

Your clients are dynamic, and so is the market. This will keep evolving and changing. And this is how Customer Experience can broaden your reach and help you cross the chasm (we'll get into that in a second). You'll reach 97% of the market instead of just focusing on the 3% that are ready to buy. You'll be playing the short and long game. You'll be playing to win.

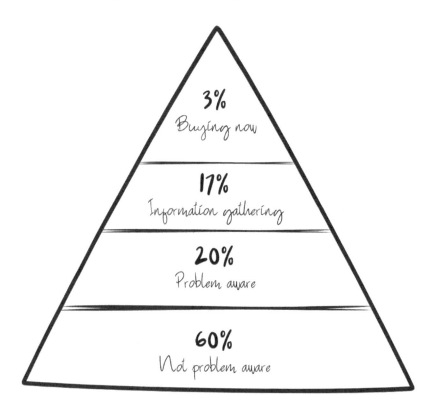

My goal is not to say forget acquisition; my goal is to remind you that you need both. When you have both you'll end up working with more Loyal Clients. Those who will stay for a long time and create a monthly recurring revenue cushion for your business.

And if I can give you some words of advice, as a business owner who has overseen more than one hundred different businesses;

run experiments and keep exploring. Our goal is not for you to stop doing what's working, but to focus on making it even better.

So after reading this book you'll end up revising your offer. I know that. It'll be more valuable, attract better clients, and have a higher LTV. But before you try to scale your business again, take a step back and look at some data.

Analyze how well your acquisition funnel is converting for the new offer, and optimize it only enough to have satisfactory results. After analyzing the acquisition funnel, you can start implementing the strategies in this book. Then you can examine how many clients are defaulting, how many are staying, and how many are successful.

If less than 5% are defaulting or looking for a competitor, you can enjoy the potential of the S-curve growth that will make your business one of a kind. You'll have plenty of Loyal clients.

A loyalty business provides lots of leverage, some of that leverage being price elasticity and premiums. You earned the right to play with prices because your reputation, success, and LTV allow that.

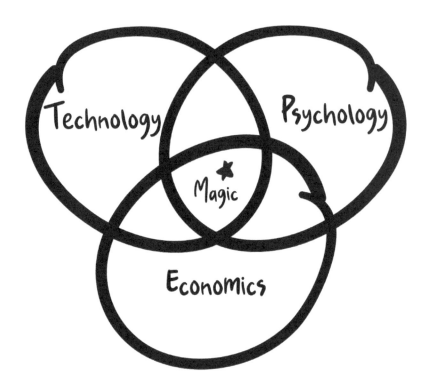

A good example to check out is one of my favorite brands: *Nespresso*.

As a very rational person, I think most things are what they are, meaning the intrinsic value is what matters. But things are not just that... things are what we compare them to. And one of the reasons I've had some bad experiences with services over the last couple of years was the low bar setting.

Expecting everything to be based on a cost-benefit analysis, ROI, and performance-driven decisions might not be the only answer. The sweet spot balances the proper mechanics, the right psychological approach, and economics.

Whenever I buy something priced "right", that delivers the intrinsic value I expected, I'm converted.

This is why I'm a Nespresso Fan.

- **Economics of Price**: it feels right, 40 cents versus a $3 Starbucks. I'm saving money.

- **Technology**: effortless, it comes in a pod, the machine is free, and any child knows how to use it.

- **Psychology**: going to the shop is the most luxurious experience. I feel like King Jay the First, where the servants are happy to serve me with a smile. They do that on purpose. You feel important.

Simple, ingenious, and beautiful.

When you see people in the online space charging super high prices, they usually charge more for the wrong reasons. It's not because the product is excellent but because their retention rate is low, the collection of payments is meager, and the only way they have to at least break even is to bump the prices and get more front-end cash. They aren't great service providers and they are playing the game wrong.

So now that you're equipped with this, let's go through one of the biggest misconceptions about fulfillment and loyalty.

Joshie the Puppet

Meet Joshie

Joshie is one of the most known stories about customer service.

It was a 'Wowing' tale about customer service.

Meet Joshie, The Puppet

Long story short, there was a kid who forgot his puppet in a Ritz-Carlton hotel. The parents called the hotel and asked if they could return it. Meanwhile, the kid thought the puppet was still enjoying vacation.

They sent it back with lots of pictures of Joshie having fun!

From that day on, that story went viral. "This is how we should do customer care."

And we love wow stories, but is this repeatable? Is this what clients are looking for?

There is a time for wow, but there is something before that. What do clients want?

1. First, they want what they paid for.

    - You may think they want wow... But wow only comes after they get the results they're looking for.

2. Second, they want ease and certainty.

    - More than wow, they want a journey with an attainable process, and they want it to be easy.

3. Third, they want it to be predictable.

    - They don't want a survivor story. They want to know this is not only achievable for them, but they can apply this to anyone they know.

4. Fourth, they want it to be affordable.

    - It doesn't mean cheap, but it should be aligned with their three most significant resources:

        i. Time

        ii. Energy

iii.　Money

Should we forget trying to over-deliver then? What is the goal of the book? What makes our clients tick?

I have some staggering numbers to share because I know numbers make what I am sharing more credible:

- 89% of businesses say they focus on exceeding expectations.

- <1% of customers say there is any difference between an expectation being met and expectations being exceeded.

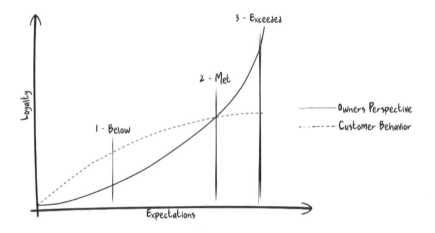

Exceeding is not the way out... But meeting expectations is. No overdelivering is needed.

It's simple, effective, and repeatable.

Equipped with this, you now know that focusing on overdelivering is not how you increase LTV or "retention."

Loyalty is much more than that. Most business owners underestimate the benefit of simply providing what was promised to customers in the first place.

And this can be achieved with the right touchpoints, helping them enjoy the journey, and by being reliable. But even those simple pieces should be delivered in a way that makes sense for your clients.

This will make them feel like your offer is reliable and predictable, effortless, and then later you can start wowing them with your company ethos.

My goal is not to make your business look like vanilla ice cream; my goal is to actually help you stand out in front of the crowd.

Most businesses that fail do so because they focus too much on the nitty-gritty and trying to impress their peers that they forget peers don't dictate their business success. Your business is a reflection of how you take care of your customers.

Your innovations aligned with giving clients what they love and avoiding what they hate will make your business successful.

Now you don't need to overhaul your business to get more Loyal customers and increase LTV. What are the benefits of having more Loyal clients in your business?

Let's find out.

Loyalty Triangle

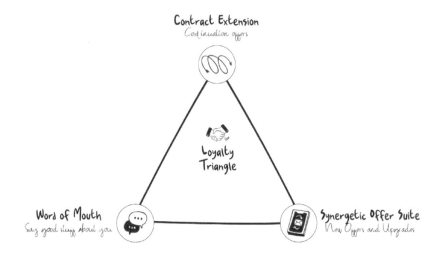

Whenever your fulfillment is working optimally, you have clients Extend their Contracts. This means they keep paying for a service they're using.

You create a Synergetic Offer Suite, where, because you have previously met their expectations, they're more willing to buy other offers you have.

And finally, the pinnacle of how to feed your ego and profit margin as a business owner: Word of Mouth. When you have great word of mouth, get referrals and testimonials, and clients that look like raving fans working for your business, Loyalty will do most of the heavy lifting for you. Now you have a client-centric business, you don't need a Cash Cow.

Why you don't need a Cash Cow to be successful

Whenever I hear the expression "make your business a cash cow," it makes me nuts, seriously. I get what people mean when they say that. But that's not what you want from your business.

Here is why…

I don't know if you're familiar with the concept of what a Cash Cow business is, but this was popularized by Richard Koch in his book the *Star Principle* (Koch is also the known author of the 80/20 Principle).

He explains how focusing on being a Cash Cow is wrong and why the goal should be becoming a Star business.

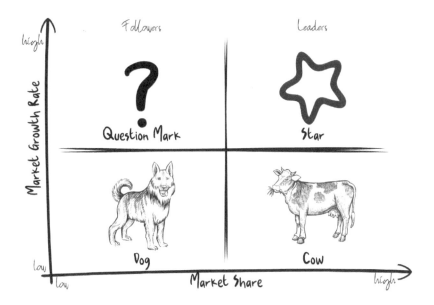

The concept says that your goal as a business owner is to ensure that your Relative Market share increases (being more dominant in the marketplace) and that the market growth rate is elevated over time. In layman's terms, there is more "need" in the market for what you offer and your building loyal clients around you.

This will help your business grow consistently at around 20% a year and it will be considered a Star Business. Yes, you don't need to trust Marketers saying that you must grow at a 100% yearly rate. If we apply some of the S-curve concepts we referred to before, some consulting companies refer to becoming not a Star but a Superstar business that can grow at a 40%+ rate yearly. Crazy, I know.

Being a Cash Cow means that the market growth rate is low, making it hard to sustain your business growth, and if your fulfillment and profit margins are low, you'll go from a Cash Cow to a Dog business.

The next challenge this brings is that if the market is growing and your relative market share is also growing, you'll cross the chasm.

Crossing the chasm is commonly used when referring to the Diffusion of Innovation, which you can see below.

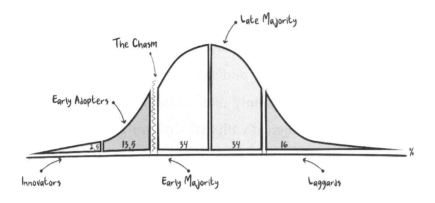

Diffusion of Innovation and Crossing the Chasm

The Diffusion of Innovation book, 1962, has proven its concepts time and time again. It was then popularized again in the book Crossing the Chasm by Geoffrey Moore.

The main takeaway to look at is that when you launch a new offer and build some momentum, you're appealing to the innovators and early adopters. These clients are extraordinary as they value being the first ones and taking risks, and they're willing to accept imperfection because they want to try it before anyone else.

These will be the clients buying your offer when you're trying to validate your idea, and they're usually great clients to work with. This is the growth phase of your business, and it's one of the most important and beautiful parts of building a business.

But if you go in the direction of building a Star Business that grows yearly, impacts more lives, and dominates your market, you'll cross the chasm eventually. And when you do, the next group of clients, the early and late majority, have a different mindset. They value certainty more than novelty, so you must ensure your offer is aligned with that. This is the maturity phase of your business, and it's the best time to scale and optimize.

If we follow the S-curve concept I introduced in the first chapter and focus on a business that can eventually become a Star (or Superstar!) business that grows and sustains that growth over time, we need something like this:

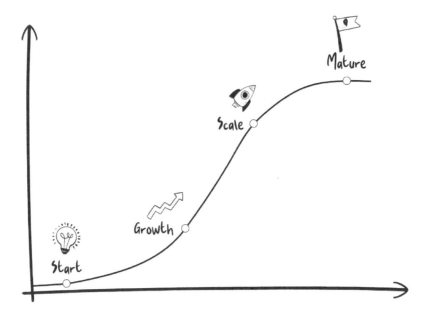

Along your business growth cycle, and while trying to Cross the Chasm, you'll find lots of inflection points. That's what we call them here. MBA students love to call them stall points, downturns, turning points, you name it. We will stick with inflection points.

For a company that has been building some momentum, trying to cross the chasm, there will be moments that require adaptation and change to keep their growth going.

When you launch a new offer, it gets some traction, and you feel great about it. It's easy to become comfortable and complacent about it. That might have happened before you decided to pick up this book.

But today, you feel things are not going as great as they once were. Maybe a new competitor is getting traction, they're selling at a cheaper price point, or people are not getting all they want from you. You feel people are becoming less interested in what you have to offer.

This couldn't have been addressed before; you didn't know what you didn't know. But now that you're aware, you can start digging and finding solutions to these challenges.

You want to keep your business in an S-curve. You want it to be profitable and to continue serving clients well while expanding to broader markets. At this point, there are only three options after the inflection point:

1. You adapt, innovate, and continue to grow.

2. You keep stagnating, chase new tactics, and things don't

improve.

3. You refuse to change, and you become obsolete.

I don't want you to get to options 2 or 3. This book aims to make customer success the best strategy for you to tackle this inflection point and to continue to grow.

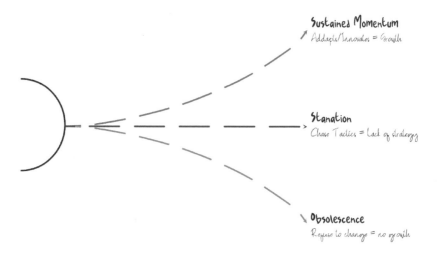

This leads me to the next point: how can you do it? That's what I will cover for the remainder of this book. When you recognize an inflection point, you need to address it:

- Make sure you're customer-centric.

- Know how to lead your team well.

- Build Customer Loyalty and Employee Loyalty.

- Keep investing in your team.

- Collect data for better decision-making.

- Reduce Environmental friction with good tools.

- Create a solid fulfillment funnel interconnected with the acquisition funnel (known as Bow-tie Funnel).

  ○ This will refine who you identify as your ideal buyer.

  ○ This will make the different departments in your business more integrated.

  ○ It'll create a more optimized customer journey.

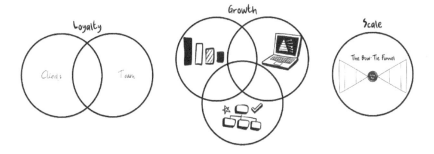

Everything that I just referred to is nothing more than relationships. Relationships like:

- Your customers with your business

- Your employees with your business

But be aware that you'll come to a fork in the road… You will only have two options.

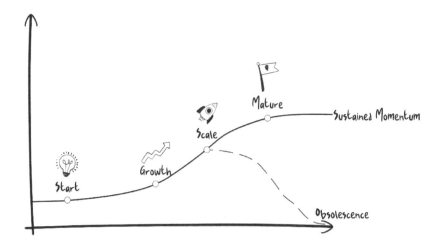

Sustained growth or obsolescence.

So if you feel like you're at an inflection point, you didn't do anything wrong. It's part of the process. But how you address it can make or break your business. If you're looking at a competitor that crossed the chasm first, you can still create a moonshot now that you'll be equipped with the psychological innovation we hone in on in this book. Don't believe me?

Let's go back to an old story about cheese. Yes, you read that right. We're discussing cheese in a Customer Success book.

Not long ago, Cheddar Cheese was sold as a truckle of cheese. This was a cylindrical wheel of cheese. But because marketers are great at finding opportunities to make it easy (reducing effort), they decided to make cheese without a rind, which is the cheese's skin.

A few years later, when a new opportunity for a new cycle

showed up, someone started a new idea, which was revolutionary: Artisan Cheddar Cheese.

This premium product was super appealing, and it was actually just: the old original cheese truckle with its rind.

Can you see how understanding your customer can give you a winning edge?

You can own the context, and context is king when you want to make your work valuable to customers. Remember, you are a product of how you make people feel. Let's make them feel great.

When competition is strong, market cycles move faster, so you need to learn how to ride the wave of competition. You'll see others trying to copy what you do, but they won't know how to create a beautiful context and experience for their clients like you do. When that happens, you can wait for the tide to go out, and customers will discover who's been swimming naked. Basically, who was overpromising and underdelivering. After they're weeded out, you can then ride the wave again.

If you feel the chasm is around the corner and your offer was working before but now it's losing traction, it's time to analyze your offer Anatomy to identify if it's built for the mass market and High LTV. We will do that in the following chapter, but have you heard of Belgo?

Belgo is a Star Business

I don't know if you drink or not, but I don't drink much. That doesn't mean that there aren't businesses that sell alcoholic beverages that aren't attractive to me.

Being a restaurant owner is a challenge, and it's not easy to be so different that people remember you more than the other guy selling the same thing.

But imagine this: you go out for dinner and enter a cavern. You find monks serving drinks in that cavern and see big steaming pots with mussels in them.

Not only is this so different from the norm, which will grab your attention, but it's also a very welcoming experience.

Belgo is a restaurant that opened in 1992 in London, and its future was never very bright. They failed several times before they were able to enjoy the perks of being a star business.

And while trying to serve better food at a lower cost was the logical solution, the owners understood the power of magic and built a psychological solution for excellent service.

The beer, the mussels, and the fries were the three things sold there. All of them had considerable margins to make this business incredible. Still, they understood that having an experience like this in a cavern served by monks would make the price irrelevant.

It was great, and the owners decided to sell it and made more than 20 times their initial investment. It pays off to create magic.

And now, let's take a look at The Economics of Scaling

Economics of Scaling

Whenever I hear the word Scaling, I get chills. It's such a misused word.

Most of the younger businesses in the online service space are still in a growth phase, and there is nothing wrong with that. But they're not Scaling.

To Scale, the economics need to play in your favor, and they need to increase the business efficiency over time.

A simple way for you to understand, whether you're already in scaling mode or still in a growth phase, is to run a calculation. How much revenue are you producing per employee?

- Let's run simple numbers and consider a business doing 1 Million dollars a year that has 10 employees. Each employee generates, on average, 100k.

- If you could scale your business in a way that you could generate the same 1 Million dollars with only 5 employees, your business productivity would double. Each employee is now able to produce, on average, 200k each. But this would require super-optimized systems to produce the same revenue with a team half the size.

- If you feel like reducing your team to half the members, let's stick to the 10 employees. And now, instead of making each employee work more to deliver the same average revenue, we work around lifetime value. If your team is now able to get your clients to stay 2x longer than they were, with the same staff and same client base, you'd be able to now produce 200k per employee on average, and your company will double from 1M to 2M a year.

These are the typical results we see with a great Fulfillment Funnel™. It's a productivity booster for any company that has gained some traction.

It's how you can double your revenue without doubling your costs. It's a profit maker.

What we typically see, is when companies go from 1M to 2 or 3M a year, they double the number of employees and other costs to accommodate this extra growth.

The company makes more revenue, but the productivity is the same at best, if not a little worse than before. Also, the company becomes more complex and harder to manage and sell.

Your goal is always to make sure that you keep simplicity for as long as you can to actually scale and not just grow your business.

You must not break your business model.

This shouldn't make you feel bad, but it will give you context to really know where you are on the diffusion of the innovation curve and how to reach broader markets.

What you need to understand next is what you are actually offering. How do you feel about your offer? What do your employees think of it?

Your offer is your reputation

I used the word offer multiple times in this book, so I want to be clear on what it means.

An offer is a clear proposal to sell or buy a specific product or service under particular conditions. Offers are made so that a reasonable person would understand it and that will result in a binding contract.

You're not reading an MBA book, so let's simplify the definition. The offer, or the offers, are what you have to sell that will solve your client's problem or problems.

That offer should consist of multiple things to allow your business to follow an S-curve, enable your business to have a successful fulfillment funnel, and build loyalty from your clients. It should consider the existing market, what your genius is and what you can deliver, and it should have some uniqueness to make it special.

Through this book, we will focus on how to make your offer unique through psychology and magic.

This book considers that you have a service that is being sold to humans, I still need to become an expert on marketing to robots, but if I ever do, I'll write another book and send it to you!

Knowing you're selling something to humans, you need to understand what they want and the problem that you're trying to solve for them.

Your clients will have two things they want to solve:

- They have Wants, which are psychological things.

- They have Needs that are typically biological or at least feel like it

Your offer should have at least one of the above, if not both. It could also be a synergetic offer suite that provides both in sequence.

To give you a simple example, our Raving Fan Formula is a consulting offer that touches on the two things above. How, you're asking?

- We cover the Wants, the psychological desire to be perceived by other business owners as successful, ethical, and a great leader for clients and team members.

- But we also address some Needs, the biological need for food and shelter that comes from the certainty they have after working with us and having solid Monthly Recurring Revenue instead of riding the Unpredictable Acquisition Rollercoaster.

And when you look at what we do, you can see how to look at your offer through a similar lens. What is your offer really delivering? What is the Big Outcome your clients want? Is it a Want? A need? A healthy mix of both?

We will have an extensive chapter explaining some of the Big Outcomes your clients might want and how to nail that for a high Lifetime Value Offer.

What's important to remember is to make your offer appeal to something immediate, what our friend Brad Newman calls a "bleeding neck problem." This changes your client's perception of solving a problem versus preventing it.

People tend to be more motivated to buy and use an offer that addresses a pain they have today versus a problem they might have in the future. This is precisely the premise we used when we started this book.

So, when you offer something that solves an immediate problem, at least the entry offer that gets your clients into your fulfillment funnel, you can begin to understand how it can be valuable to them.

Also, if this offer solves a problem, it means that after that problem is solved, there will be new problems they need to be aware of and will need help fixing. This is why when we consult with a client, we work on The Profit Multiplier, which is the work done to build a synergetic offer suite that connects the new problem to a new solution that creates or connects to the desire for your clients to stay with you for longer.

So now that you know a little more of an understanding about your offer, how you can shape your reputation and a little explanation about its perceived value, how can you look at the market and understand exactly what you've been offering and why clients want it?

You will have different markets that desire various offers depending on where they are regarding their needs. I don't know if you are familiar with Maslow's Pyramid of Needs, but I'm going to use a simplified version to explain what I mean:

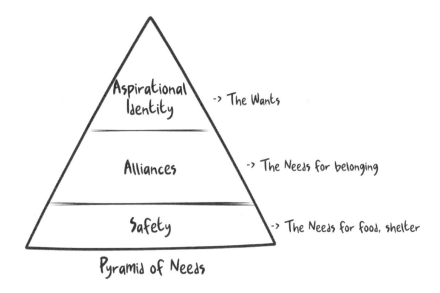

Pyramid of Needs

Looking at the above, you can see that the higher the income your clients make, the more they will be looking for alliances and Aspirational Identity. Also, the opposite applies. The lower the income, the more they look for safety.

Just look at how people behave. Most humans who feel they're struggling will overreact because it means they're in a binary mindset. They either feel successful or like a loser.

It's important to understand where your clients are regarding their needs because they'll only follow their dreams (what we will call Aspirational Identity) after they feel like they're not in survival mode anymore.

And this is the largest difference between Wants and Needs.

When someone is above "safety," they chase the Wants, the

vanity, the transcendence, if you will.

When they feel below "safety," they're in survival mode and pursue what they believe they need to survive.

Understanding how your offer connects with your client's Needs is essential because if they don't have their Needs covered, they won't want to chase something greater. Your client's Needs can be one or a mix of:

- **Resources**: food, shelter, money.

- **Alliances**: belonging, love, connection.

- **Trust**: self-esteem and self-confidence.

Understanding the above, and what you really offer, gives you a chance to properly position your offer to the market, while giving you more leverage in holding clients accountable to their Needs and Wants.

If you feel like your clients are struggling with resources, find a quick way to help them get more of those. If they're struggling with alliances and have low self-esteem, make them feel connected with you or some of their peers. If they're working with trust, you can support them in a way that can increase their confidence in themselves.

What is significant about the above is that it's all based on a client's perception. This is why some millionaires feel like they are still in survival mode. Even though they have money, they also have perceived scarcity.

Equipped with the information about how your offer fits within your client's psychology, you need to understand what your offer does. Are you helping your clients Repair something or Replace it?

Alen Sultanic's explanation gave me one of the biggest epiphanies I've had when looking at offers.

When you think about Repairing something, it means it's an offer that fixes something that is broken for your clients. Something they are super invested in and that they want to hang onto due to sunk cost bias. In the following chapters, I will explain in detail what sunk cost means and how you can use it for better client engagement.

Repairing something that is broken can be simple. If your clients are running ads for their Acquisition Funnel and everything is underperforming, and you offer them a solution that lowers their acquisition costs, you're repairing their system. It's a bleeding neck problem.

If you look at what we do with the Raving Fan Formula, our clients typically have high acquisition costs, little to no retention of clients, contracts that are, on average, not even 90 days, and a team that is burning out. They need that Repaired, or their business will crumble.

But your offer can also be a Replacement option for your clients. If they're tired of what they have in place and looking for completely new opportunities, they might want to replace everything they have.

This usually applies to an early stage of what they're doing, and because they're not committed, it's easy to quit, call it a day, and replace it with something new.

Let me give you two examples of the above, one for a B2B (business to business) offer and one for a B2C (business to customer) offer.

Imagine your clients hire someone to help them build a digital marketing agency. They have some success, but they're so overworked that they start losing hope of the promise of a 4-hour workweek. They will blame that business, or maybe Tim Ferris.

And then, they see your offer, which helps them replace their business model with a Done With You offer. Instead of doing everything for clients, they coach, guide, and teach clients how to do it themselves. You helped them Replace their existing model.

But this also applies to selling to customers directly. If someone started a keto diet, and they need to be more successful and get better results, they want to replace that system. They hire you to help them set up a flexible diet approach where they can eat everything in moderation. You sold them a complete Replacement.

The above doesn't give you an actionable solution, but it will create some context for you to remember who's being served by your offer.

Now it's time to break it down into different components and its perceived value for clients. Your offer is clear. You know who you serve, the purpose, and why they want it. How can you make it a moonshot and increase its value 10x? That's what you will learn in the following chapter.

Takeaways

Now that we're on the same page in terms of looking at your business for maximum performance and profitability, you will start seeing fulfillment and client success as another source of revenue.

If you have a fulfillment process in place now, you have already started this work. Your goal will be to make it simpler, more reliable, and more efficient while making your team the best system users.

Your team will use this playbook daily to serve clients at the highest level. This will be your manual for Relationships at Scale.

You don't need to lower your lead cost with all this in place. You don't need to force the Sales team to sell to more people who're not a great fit because, with the uptick in client LTV, you have more flexibility when it comes to the cost of acquisition.

Summary:

- A streamlined fulfillment system is the easiest way to generate extra revenue with no acquisition costs.

- The Fulfillment funnel is typically ignored, and aligning it with the Acquisition funnel helps create a Bow-Tie funnel.

- Performance Marketing is the simplest to measure (direct-response) but is often shortsighted.

- Loyal clients will spread good word of mouth and get more eyes on your offers.

- The simplest way to having Raving Fans it is to meet the client's expectations.

- All of the above will help your offer cross the chasm.

The increased loyalty, LTV, referrals, and reduced dropouts and refunds, will put you in an Empowered and profitable State.

But is this achievable for any business or any client? Well, yes and no, it depends on how your offer is perceived by your customers.

III. HIGH LTV OFFERS

"Not everything that makes sense works, and not everything that works makes sense."

Rory Sutherland

Anatomy of a High LTV Offer

Offers dictate a lot of a business's success. They make marketing attractive, sales smooth, and fulfillment an easy-peasy job.

The problem is that offers can't be oversimplified around the tangible deliverables or expected intrinsic value. We probably shouldn't just trust what clients say they want.

People don't think what they feel, don't say what they believe, and don't do what they say.

Your offer will dictate where you're going. The offer will be critical in crossing the chasm or not, to enable an S-curve idea to grow and see people adopt it. But don't get me wrong, this is not achievable with a single shot. This will require a lot of work and iteration over time.

It might even require you to reinvent yourself along the way, in order for you to get closer to where you want to be.

Your offer is a little bit of you, but it has the soul of your team as well. You must keep that in mind, as you want your team members to show up like Brasilata Employees.

Brasilata is a Brazilian company that produces cans, and they were inspired by Japanese manufacturers like Honda and Toyota, which empower their employees to take ownership of their work.

In 1987, Brasilata launched an employee-innovation program after they saw what was working for the Japanese companies.

The program's goal was to change employees' identities, so they became known as inventors as soon as they joined the company. They even signed an innovation contract. And all employees were challenged to find ideas to make better products, improve processes, and even remove unnecessary delivery costs.

The now-known program produced 134,846 ideas, for an average of 145.2 ideas per "inventor."

When your team is empowered with the right tools, they'll feel good about making the offer better and creating opportunities for everyone's good.

Remember I said before that you'll have several inflection points in your offer and not just one? Those inflection points can be addressed individually, but in the following chapters, we'll give you enough frameworks to tackle most of them if you have a service-based business.

Together we will use psychological solutions to provide you with the best and most promising approach possible while keeping clients excited and happy. But why would you go the route of creating a psychological solution for your clients? Because you can have a magical moonshot offer on your hands.

I want a moonshot, you want a moonshot, and everyone wants a moonshot offer. We want what we do to increase 10x in value and make us the most successful entrepreneurs on planet earth. That's how you build a Star or maybe even a Superstar business.

Moonshot meaning:

This use of moonshot refers to a project or venture intended to have deep-reaching or outstanding results after one heavy, consistent, and usually quick push.

But as Rory Sutherland said several times, creating a 10x moonshot offer is much easier using psychological improvements than technological enhancements. There is a technical limitation of how you can make your offer 10x better on the skill set approach, but there are no limits to the psychological breakthroughs. We don't want to make trains 10x faster, first because it's not easy as it was in the nineteen twenties, but we can still make the train journey much more enjoyable.

Here is the explicit difference between this book and what we've seen done in the online service world before.

We will use an undefeated solution to create Raving Fans in your business: psychology and relationships.

Some business owners think that psychological improvements could be deceptive or misleading. I'm afraid I have to disagree with this and agree with the statement that magic is hard in the physical world, but it's very doable in the psychological world. That's what we do when watching superheroes in a movie or reading a novel. We're creating magic in our minds.

I'm not saying this is easy, but it exists. Think about Uber's story and how a psychological moonshot can be implemented with ease and great success.

The story says that Uber's creator watches the James Bond movie Goldfinger, and in the film, James Bond can follow the car of Goldfinger, in real-time, on a screen map in his Aston Martin while driving through Switzerland.

This idea created a lightbulb moment for Uber's future, the inclusion of a map.

Before Uber, people suffered when calling for a cab, unsure if it was coming or not, confused if they missed the location, and waiting under three feet of snow to make sure they could be seen!

Uber tapped into that uncertainty feeling with a psychological moonshot: adding a map that shows precisely where the driver is at any time and knowing how long it will take to arrive at their destination. Uber didn't try to make the wait shorter or the ride faster. They focused on removing stress and uncertainty to make the experience pleasant. They made a cab ride predictable.

Uber doesn't stop there though, they also add status. Leaving your house and having a fancy car waiting for you makes you feel like a star. If you had to wait for a cab under heavy rain, you'd feel like an average Joe, and it would be a low-status experience.

Predictability is one of the most important psychological triggers for humans. I will go deeper into that in the application chapter, where I talk about the power of a predictable journey and how to map your offer touchpoints and deliver a great experience.

And that experience doesn't need to be a straight line and full of emotional highs. As humans, we tend to ignore the duration of incidents but remember a few particular moments (I will go down the rabbit hole on how this works in the Bonus Section).

As an engineer, I love using a good old equation to explain what I mean by perceived value, psychological breakthroughs, and a high lifetime value offer. Alex Hormozi came up with the best and most straightforward explanation I've seen to date:

This equation is fully aligned with my perspective on value and I was mind blown the first time I read his 100M Offers book . A psychological approach to creating perceived value makes the client feel an offer is more valuable.

This is very relevant as there are some misconceptions about the meaning of intrinsic value. None of us value things based on what they are but on what they mean to us. And all that is valuable to us will be context-dependent, which makes this psychological approach so exciting and practical for the customer. We're embedding meaning.

But what does this mean? How can you understand the way your clients perceive value? Here are a few key components:

- How big is the outcome?

  - This is your big promise, the outcome of your offer.

- ○ Consider this number a 0-100

- ○ Where 0 is a promise that keeps them where they are, and 100 gets them to their big life goal.

- How realistic is it for them to achieve the outcome?

  - ○ This is the belief they have aligned with the big promise.

  - ○ We consider this value binary, 0 or 1

  - ○ Where 0 means they don't believe the goal is attainable, and 1 means they think it is possible

- How much time would it take for them to achieve?

  - ○ Also known as speed to results, how long will it take for them to be at the big promise and outcome?

  - ○ We consider this number to go from 0-∞

  - ○ Where 0 means as soon as they pay, they get the big promise and ∞ means they would never get that big outcome.

- How much effort do they need to put in to get to the big outcome?

  - ○ Also known as the perception of effort, which doesn't always mean the exertion needed to get to the big promise.

- ○ We consider this number to go from 0-∞

- ○ Where 0 means they need to put little effort to get what they want and ∞ means they would need to hustle and grind to inhumane levels to get to where they want to go.

I know it sounds a bit mathematical, but I'm an Engineer at heart, so it's hard for me not to give you numbers to aim for. Whenever the client's perceived value from your offer is high, you end up with high LTVs and retention.

What should your goals based on the equation above? You should focus on playing with the ingredients that will give you the best bang for your buck.

Here is a quick engineering tip before we get into the nitty-gritty:

- When working with fractions, the result is zero if the top number is equal to zero.

  - ○ This means that if the big outcome is 0 for your client, in other words, they stay where they are, they perceive zero value from your offer.

  - ○ Also, if the belief is 0, they don't believe the goal is attainable. They perceive zero value from your offer.

- If the top number is as high as possible, the fraction gets its maximum result from the top numbers.

  ○ If the big outcome is 100, getting your client to the life goal they want, they perceive great value from your offer.

  ○ Also, if the belief is 100, they believe the goal is attainable and perceive value from your offer.

- When working with fractions, if the bottom number is equal to zero, the result is ∞

  ○ If the time to get the big promise is 0 (immediately), they will perceive the maximum value from the offer.

  ○ Also, if the perception of effort is 0, they feel like they are not putting in any effort and will perceive maximum value from the offer.

- If the bottom number is ∞, the fraction gets its value close to 0

  ○ This means that if the time they need to get to the big outcome is ∞, the perceived value will be 0

  ○ Also, if the effort needed to get the big outcome is ∞, the perceived value will be 0.

Can you see something here? Patterns?

Most marketers focus so much on the top part, promising more, brainwashing their prospects that crazy goals are doable that they end up being known for having a scam offer.

The bottom part has been forgotten, which is why the Customer Success Manifesto will change the game for you.

This should be your new recipe:

Let's go ingredient by ingredient, like a Master Chef.

Big Outcome

I'll start with a big idea:

"Once we move beyond the simple satisfaction of our needs, we move into the complex world of satisfying our wants."

This was well said by Seth Godin in his book *All Marketers Are*

Liars, and it changed how I look at any offer, especially the Big Outcome.

Let's look at what I mean by Big Outcome. This is not simple. Not a number. It's something else. But what is it?

Let's start with what it isn't. The Big Outcome is not the tangible promise or what people call intrinsic value. That's only the surface level, where all the competition is.

People only have to address the apparent tangible promise by going with technical solutions that address the obvious, like what the British and French did when working around rebuilding the Eurostar train that connects Paris to London.

That project spent around 6 billion pounds to reduce the journey by approximately 20 minutes because the goal was to address customers' needs: a faster journey.

The journey is now roughly two hours and fifteen minutes after a meager investment of 6 billion pounds.

What this team missed was what customers wanted... Comfort and a great experience.

Spending 0.1% of that budget to give passengers free wi-fi would have made the experience great while costing almost nothing.

If they went all in, they could spend 10% of that budget and pay all the best female and male models in the world to roam around the trains providing people with complimentary drinks during their trip. And I bet people would ask for a slower train and a longer trip!

It's funny to observe all these engineers, faulty like I am, trying to solve problems with a linear approach. They didn't actually add free wi-fi access until ten years and 6 billion pounds later.

The problem with this "eyes-on-the-prize" mentality is that it creates too much attachment to tangible outcomes and people tend to be overconfident about how easy it is to be self-disciplined to get to where they want to be. This keeps people thinking about a surface problem.

Thinking about the surface problem isn't enough. When you think about the Big Outcome, it should be something that gets your client closer to their Aspirational Identity. They've always dreamed of experiencing a certain kind of life, but they're not quite there yet. This is where people can experience financial and time freedom, the status they get from all their success, and provide their families with what they deserve.

This is pivotal when considering your offer's perceived value because if the meaning behind the Big Outcome you're promising goes against the experience they want from life, you'll face friction and eventually your clients will stop taking action.

For example, imagine your client says he wants to live a life of time freedom, where working four hours a day is the maximum he's willing to commit. That's what you're selling, so they love it and buy it.

But as soon as they do, the first thing you ask them to do is to work more hours, non-stop, seven days a week. This primary friction point makes the process feel like it's not aligned with the idea of their dream life. What they really want to do is embody an Aspirational Identity that was subconsciously sold to them.

This Aspirational Identity promises the great experience they can have after achieving the Big Outcome you promised.

That Aspirational Identity might not be apparent, as it's usually a deeper level of understanding of who we are serving. When selling someone on the Big Outcome, we give them a weapon to destroy a common evil. We're joining forces to fight what had been keeping them stuck. Us vs. Them.

So when thinking about the Big Outcome, the offer's perceived value, and how to connect all those dots across marketing, sales, and fulfillment, you must go a few layers deeper.

The Story Brand book, which I'll go into further detail on in the following chapters, states that all customers face three common problems:

1. **External Problems**

    a. Often something tangible that a hero must face to

save the day.

b. Commonly these are the 3-5 symptoms they feel weekly and that they're aware of, that you're probably already using in your marketing materials and sales process.

2. **Internal Problems**

a. Have you heard "people buy on emotion and justify with logic"? If so, we can translate it as people buy because of internal problems and justify it based on external ones.

b. Remember, what frustration your service solves. Reassure them about that, and it'll increase the perceived value.

c. If you can tie together internal and external problems, and if the service solves both, you increase the perceived value.

3. **Philosophical Problems**

a. The philosophical problem is typically found in customer statements like "shouldn't."

b. *"High ticket programs shouldn't only focus on revenue."*

c. How can you involve the customer in a story that's

bigger than themselves? How can you tie the outcome together with the Aspirational Identity?

d. This makes them more motivated and the offer exponentially more valuable. This can be considered the perfect psychological moonshot.

Think about Tesla and how the Electric Vehicle industry has been doing this for a while now. They found a common evil, saying that all cars have inferior technology.

Positioning Electric Vehicles using this framework:

- **External Problem:** I need a new car

- **Internal Problem:** I want to be an early adopter of new technology (diffusion of innovation again!)

- **Aspirational Identity:** I want to help save the environment

So whenever your Big Outcome keeps reminding them about who they want to be, the perceived value sticks. This creates expectancy about what their life will look like and how their friends will talk about them.

That Big Outcome is just a simplification of what they want to live; it's an Aspirational Identity. And in order for your clients to feel like they're living that life, you need to create some feedback loops that highlight that.

Not only does this help with perceived value, but it will feed the most crucial feedback to our Marketing and Sales team to speak the right language to our pre-clients. So when you think about this Aspirational Identity, you need to think about your clients' internal and philosophical problems. Thinking about your client and offering: what could be a problem that is keeping them far away from the Aspirational Identity they want to embody?

You need to address variables individually if you want a high perceived value and a high LTV offer. Here are some examples of typical desires or some internal problem that connects with the Aspirational Identity:

- **Conserving financial resources,** for example, they may need to save money. When working with a Financial Advisor the first steps could be to cut back spending so that you can have resources to attain your future financial goals. Or an Agency assisting a business to run ads to get cheaper leads, better close rates, and more profitability with less ad spend.

- **Conserving time,** for example, they may want to save time to spend time doing other things they love. This is the typical "4-hour work week" message and why it worked so well. It's based on time freedom.

- **Building social networks,** as an example, if the brand helps them find a community and a tribe, you have a powerful hook. I love using CrossFit as the perfect example of how you can charge a premium, injure your customers, and still have people love what you do… with the power of belonging to a tribe.

- **Gaining status**, as an example of luxury brands, gaining status taps into this human need to keep clients happy (and status means new allies). Did you see that guy with a Lambo? He's looking for status.

- **Accumulating resources,** if the service helps people make more money or gather resources, we shall remind the client about the desire. This is the typical "get rich quick" messaging we see online nowadays.

- **The innate desire to be generous:** When your clients want to achieve an aspirational identity, the innate desire to be generous helps other people survive; this desire can be compelling. This internal urge to give back is slightly different from just accumulating resources, which is one reason wealthy people love to contribute to Charities and Foundations with a purpose.

- **The desire for meaning**: When your business allows your clients to be part of something bigger than themselves, you have a philosophy for them to live. This happens when the student becomes the teacher and wants to do the same for others.

I like to keep the things above in mind when I think about the Big Outcome; there could be more and different angles to look at. Let me sprinkle a couple examples that can be tested for new offers you come up with after reading this book. Here is how you can connect your offers to the big meaning I shared around the Aspirational Identity:

- **Novelty**, you can be selling something new that no one is selling.

- **Certainty**, if you can guarantee results that no one else can.

- **Automation**, if you can save their time doing boring things.

- **F.O.M.O.**, if you have an offer that has an expiration date.

- **You**, if it can help them become the person they want to be by hanging out with you.

Something to keep in mind is that now that you understand what you're selling, don't try to sell everything at once. Not only does it make your offer more complex, but it also makes the journey longer for clients. It could also easily be another offer that addresses different Needs and Wants your clients has or will have. Your offer should solve ONE problem, with ONE solution; if they need more because they have a NEW problem, sell ANOTHER solution.

Now that you understand the outcome is much more than promising a client he'll make a million dollars, you'll have a lot more leverage in your marketing, sales and in your delivery process working with clients.

Do you understand the significance behind what is promised to your prospects and what makes them buy? Now I bet you do.

But do your clients believe the outcome is possible for them? Let's find out.

Perceived Likelihood of Achievement

All actions are belief-driven. Right? Imagine you wanted to lose a couple of pounds, you've been moving less and eating more, and your sweatpants are getting tighter.

How will you make sure you lose those pounds for good? The options are endless, but you must first believe the outcome is possible.

I remember we were finishing a retreat for a few business owners. Ben had one of his epiphanies, which he'll share in a sec.

Ben, please take the reins.

I was scrolling Facebook, and a post smacked me in the face. It was my soon-to-be coach describing exactly how I felt about my physical body. Let's just say the feelings weren't positive.

Not only had I gained forty pounds over nine years, but I felt tremendous guilt since I said in my personal training days that I would never let myself get fat.

I knew what I had to do. I reached out to the coach who made that post and signed up with him. He was like, 'don't you want to get on a call first?' I respected that because he wanted to make sure he could help me. But I had seen his work over the years and knew it was time.

That was eight months ago. I've lost thirty pounds of fat and gained ten pounds of muscle by consistently implementing the simple system this coach teaches.

But it hasn't been easy. A few months ago, I felt stuck. I stayed at the same weight for two months. Now, I understand that the number on the scale doesn't always change, but I didn't feel like I was progressing.

My coach made some adjustments, and I dug into my desire to be in peak shape. It worked. I began to lose again, but more importantly, the mirror started telling me the story I wanted to hear.

When I struggled, I had to check my thinking and actions and ask for help. I got back to believing the outcome was possible for me…

When I looked at Ben, I could see something magical happening: his belief in what's possible changed. He was full of hope again.

Whenever you look at the perceived value equation, you need to remember that the belief part is binary, so you either believe it or not. If you want to have a high perceived value offer, you should:

- Engineer hope and future pace so your clients can see the big outcome.

  - Your clients don't want to believe this happened once with a client, but that this process you have is repeatable. Once this happens, they'll trust you more and refer more people because they know it works for others too.

  - When you cross the chasm, and your offer grows to more than innovators and early adopters, these types of clients value certainty, so they'll be measuring their level of certainty that dictates the belief they have about the goal being attainable.

  - When dealing with clients, one of the best ways to get them to believe the goal is attainable is to focus on the relationship side, this is what we call Experience Engineering, and this is why this book will teach team to do that (using behavioral economics, psychology, and experience)

- When working around the belief part, you want to make sure your clients can connect the dots.

- Your main goal is to connect the long-term, Big Outcome with short-term critical moves. This will help them understand why they're doing what they're doing.

- Belief is not static, and it can change over time. As you probably noticed, a client might believe the outcome is doable after a great sales call, but whenever they start the process, they stop taking action or seeing any value from the work because they stop believing it. They'll regret the decision.

- You need to understand the MOTs.

  - MOT stands for Moment of Truth

  - Those inflection points can make or break the relationship.

  - Your offer should have at least 3-5 MOTs that should be mapped out, anticipated, and communicated to the client to avoid disbelief.

  - Remember, every interaction tells the story of your product or service's quality, sophistication, and value. Treat each interaction as an opportunity to make clients believe it's worth it.

And now, let's talk about time.

Time Delay

For humans, time is not measured in seconds. Time is measured in how they **perceive** time. This can be measured in pain, boredom, or irritation, not seconds.

Let's look at this study run by David Eagleman from Stanford on the perception of time. In the study he asked participants to leap off a 150-foot platform and free fall into a net.

Then after that, he asked people to describe how long the fall took, and the estimates were, on average, too high by 36%. The fear and extra focus during the experience caused an expansion of time. And you know this, right? Look at the English language.

If you look at the basis of the English language, we say things like "time flies while having fun" or "it was the longest 10 minutes of my life". This describes how we perceive time.

This is one of the most challenging parts of the perceived value equation. As you know, an offer has multiple ingredients that are interconnected, so when you play with one, you affect the others.

People can't predict the future. Have you tried to imagine yourself 10 years from now? Is that person in your mind an older version of you or just a stranger?

Several studies show that we can't always see our future selves as ourselves, and we might see that person more like someone else.

That's interesting and explains why we're so wired to get results in the present, also called present bias.

Humans have a non-linear perception of time, meaning we don't operate like your laptop clock. This is why you feel like time sometimes passes faster and other times slower. That's a psychological component we can tap into to make the experience of your offer more enjoyable.

Waiting is not made for us, and this explains why we're wired for instant gratification and not so much for what requires delayed gratification. I prefer ten dollars today instead of eleven dollars one year from now!

But there is something else around the idea of wanting things now, something even more powerful that comes from an ancestral part of our brain: It´s certainty.

I shared Uber's story, where the map gave the customer the certainty to value the service more, and you can tap into the same psychological moonshot when reviewing your high LTV offer.

If you feel like your clients don't love taking risks and don't want to wait to get a Big Outcome that takes a lot of time, you can tap into playing with the outcome and make the result happen faster.

If you try to speed the time to result, play with the safe choice and offer your clients certainty and predictability.

Going back to the perceived value equation, you want Time Delay to be as close to zero as possible to increase the offer's perceived value. But I see some bold and outrageous offers out there being run by marketers with outcomes that are not only unrealistic, but the time needed to get there will be so long that people will stop believing it's even worth the effort.

So to play with the Time Delay, you might need to play with the promised Big Outcome to make it realistic and get the results faster – That's the safe bet I just talked about.

Another alternative is, if the offer requires a really Big Outcome to be sellable, help the client focus on a significant partial result that makes them feel closer to the outcome they want and make sure that partial result happens very fast.

Early success is a form of engineering hope that is the best fuel for clients who struggle with taking action.

As you observe time in a non-linear manner, you can change your client's perception of time to keep them engaged. This can allow you to reframe the time needed to get to the Big Outcome, not as waiting but as preparation time.

You can frame milestones as a preparation cycle for your perfect customer to truly benefit from on their journey to hitting the Big Outcome.

There are some caveats to understand when it comes to being fast to results that we will discuss, in a second, in the effort component.

Effort

Effort follows a similar logic to Time Delay. You want it to be as close to zero as possible to ensure the offer feels super valuable.

There are, of course, tradeoffs and a balance to be found on the Effort side. If it's too much, it reduces the perceived value of the offer, but too little can reduce sunk cost bias and make them less committed because it's too easy. Humans, they're amazing.

We will discuss the sunk cost effect and application later in the book.

I love stories, so let's look at another. You go to IKEA, navigate through the maze, find that new desk for your office, spend a couple of hundred dollars, spend an afternoon working through the puzzle, and now you're a proud IKEA employee. Maybe not, but close.

You think your masterpiece looks incredible. This is called the IKEA effect.

If you google it:

"The IKEA effect is a cognitive bias in which consumers place a disproportionately high value on partially-created products. The name refers to Swedish manufacturer and furniture retailer IKEA, which sells many items of furniture that require assembly."

So Effort will be a bit of art to ensure we remove unnecessary effort, but we keep enough effort for customers to be actively engaged.

The second example of this comes from a story about a food processing firm that marketed a cake mix that required the housewife to add only water to produce a creamy batter and perfect cake.

The company could not understand why the mix would not sell until careful research revealed that the public felt uneasy about a mix that required only water. It seemed too simple.

They felt they had to do something for it to feel like a real cake mix. The company changed the formula and required the housewife to add an egg. Immediately, the combination achieved great success. A little bit of Effort goes a long way.

Getting back to the perceived value, the offers some marketers are making today are so outrageous that not only does the client need time to get there, but the client also needs an enormous amount of Effort that is unsustainable.

So in order to tackle the perception of Effort, you need to play with the Big Outcome from a meaningful perspective which will make the whole value equation much simpler.

But even if you don't play with anything else, you can do a couple of things to reduce the perceived Effort or at least avoid unnecessary effort and friction.

Here is what you could do to reduce the perception of Effort:

- Remove as much unnecessary Effort as possible across the customer journey with you.

- Whenever possible, make the process feel effortless and aligned with the three core resources:

    o Time

    o Energy

    o Money

- If the process of working with you is easy, they don't need more support to get unstuck. Make your program a guided self-service experience.

- Whenever a client is feeling friction and asks for support, don't focus solely on the problem they have now. Take time to help them get unstuck, but also address any other future issues you know they'll face so they're better equipped to keep moving forward.

- Avoid Environmental Friction:

  o Fix the user experience challenges and find any step in your offer, website, or tech stack that creates more friction than necessary.

  o Avoid SPOF (Single Point of Failure). This was one of my biggest learnings as an engineer.

  o When you think about SPOF, you want all the customer paths to have redundancy and/or a contingency plan.

  o Working on SPOFs will require radical truth and transparency about your offering; you might find holes, and you should learn from them so you can make your program better over time.

- Avoid Rational Friction:

- ○ Reduce cognitive load, ensuring nothing is confusing so clients don't feel friction due to the lack of clarity and can take action immediately.

- ○ Make sure you always have LOS (Line of Sight). From my Engineering days, one of the most significant pieces of the puzzle was when planning my delivery and interactions with clients or how the system was delivered. You should always know what comes next, and there should be no blind spots.

- Emotional friction:

  - ○ The hardest thing to remove from all three types of friction. The best you can do is to empower your clients to take action while understanding their goals' real meaning.

To solve the emotional friction part, the upcoming archetypes section will give you all you need.

High LTV Offer Clinic

I'll take an inception approach for this clinic and explain how we organized our consulting offer using all of the ingredients explained.

- How big is the outcome?

  - Our clients have big dreams. Usually a mix of being part of a great community of peers, making enough money to have a very relaxed life, and having the time freedom to not work every day of the week. They want to escape the sleepless nights thinking about client drop-offs and short contracts that don't allow them to create monthly recurring revenue and want to trust their team to work with clients effectively.

  - We keep that in mind when working with them, and when we work on something, we make sure the owner doesn't get buried under more work. We help them launch other offers that can increase profitability while making retention better to keep more clients for longer.

- How realistic is it for them to achieve the outcome?

  - Our clients believe this is possible. They've seen others doing it before.

  - This makes our life easier. We don't need to convince our clients that effectively delegating delivery to their team, extending their contracts by 4x, and increasing profitability will create the business they want.

- How much time would it take for them to achieve the result?

  - ○ Fulfillment work can be challenging as it's like the 8th wonder of the world, compound interest. Our goal is not to help them skyrocket their business overnight but to change the most relevant pieces that will create exponential growth over time.

  - ○ That being said, we audit everything early on to find some easy wins that can be implemented immediately that usually generate more revenue, more time for the owner, and a happier team.

- What is their perception of effort?

  - ○ Our client is a business owner that's already busy, so we focus on working with a team when they have one or being precise on what work needs to be done with the owner.

  - ○ So instead of making our consulting clients suffer, we work on our delivery to make it simple and easy for them while providing the quick wins and momentum they need to keep going.

Quite simple, right? Now it's your turn.

Do It Yourself

Please use the High LTV Offers worksheet so you can review this chapter yourself and apply your big takeaways to your business and offers.

Click or go to the website: https://ethicalscaling.com/csm-book-downloads/

Scan me to download

Takeaways

Churn and Burn is exhausting; it's easy to get swept up in how 'others' are doing business. Making big promises in marketing and sales to lure clients in, but then falling short of meeting those expectations on the back end is very common.

You may have experienced this yourself. And this makes you think, 'we need to over-deliver, and I won't rest until we do.'

I get it. You want to stay true to your word.

But I have something to lighten the weight of your expectations.

All you have to do is two things:

1. Understand your client's expectations

2. Meet those expectations

We have done this with more than a hundred six, seven, and eight-figure clients when implementing the Raving Fan Formula. When you create the best experience for your customers from day one, they'll rave about you forever.

Our approach is both a psychological and practical process that guides you through creating and providing the best possible experience for your customers. By providing a perfect customer journey–clients will be happy to pay to work together and stay longer. Extending their lifetime value, increasing your reputation, and hitting new levels of profitability.

Summary:

- The offer and how innovative it is from the client's perspective will dictate the success of your business in the long term.

- There are four significant ingredients: Big Outcome, Likelihood of Achievement, Time Delay, and Effort.

- Big Outcome is not only the tangible result they get from the offer. There's also the Aspirational Identity they look forward to embodying.

- Likelihood of Achievement is how much they believe the Big Outcome to be possible and either drives them into action or inaction.

- Time delay is non-linear and can feel longer or shorter depending on how excited or anxious they are about the process.

- Effort should be based on their perception and not what you think is the actual exertion, and it should be kept within a healthy range due to the IKEA effect to keep clients engaged.

IV. THE FULFILLMENT CONTINUUM

"Give one person responsibility for listening to your customers, and authority to act on what they hear."

Guy Letts

That one guy

I opened my messenger and had several messages from different people and my phone wouldn't stop buzzing from notifications.

Clients were reaching out, panicking. Did the world end? I was confused.

They were all asking why things weren't working for them...They were trying their best to get the results we promised them with the process we gave, but they were in a mental block.

I started sweating and overthinking, second-guessing my skills as a coach and that my service maybe wasn't as excellent as I bragged about it being. It still gives me chills thinking about it.

All of them asked me to jump on a call to spoon-feed them or get a refund. It wasn't working for them.

I was already stretched too thin; having more calls on my calendar that week was impossible, and if I left them waiting, my collections for split-pay clients would have been zero that month, if I was lucky.

I opened up my calendar as I needed to support my clients. Integrity is essential to me. It's one of my core values.

I started twelve-hour days, seven days a week, burning myself out. Clients weren't happy. I made an exception for ad-hoc calls, but they didn't see it as valuable.

Some didn't show up on time, and others did, but it looked like we weren't speaking the same language.

Others were on the edge of quitting their dream forever. It was nerve-wracking.

I felt like I was repeatedly pushing a boulder back to the top of the mountain.

The Sisyphus Tale

Keep pushing the boulder...

Imagine a simple scenario:

I give you a boulder that you need to push up a mountain. As soon as you reach the top, it rolls down again. It looks like a curse, an absurd and meaningless task that you will repeat forever.

This was Sisyphus's curse for cheating death twice. And sometimes, when an online service business's fulfillment system is broken, it feels like a Sisyphean task.

I continually see business owners, who reach out to us for help, suffer from this never-ending curse of pushing the boulder up the mountain repeatedly.

Owners often tell us "I will work on my fulfillment and systems as soon as I bring in some more revenue."

They almost reach the top (more revenue), and the boulder rolls down again.

That's exactly how I felt and how I could have still been feeling today. Thankfully, I sorted it out.

It doesn't need to be like that. You can either spread your energy and attention all over the place or focus on what will bring you results.

It can stop. It is up to you. You're the one in charge.

In today's hyper-connected and hyper-competitive business world, old ways of providing customer service are failing.

With emerging tech and big data, most business owners thought that the surveys and market research around Voice of Customer (VoC) and Customer Relationship Management (CRM) alone would change how we do business and help to engineer exceptional experiences across the customer journey. But it doesn't.

See, you're not that special. Well, you are, but your clients don't know that yet.

"They don't care how much you know until they know how much you

care."

They can buy anything, anywhere, anytime, across a wide range of prices and quality. Keep that in mind.

You need to stand out and think outside the box. This is why we're here. And this will be done using unique human experiences facilitated by your business. In the next few years, the allure of shiny objects will decrease as buyers become more and more savvy, and the most successful companies will be focused on innovation around customer experience.

Why? Because of the considerable power shift that has already started happening. The control has moved from business owners to the customers.

The Ideal Customer Engineer

As an owner, you might come up with your offerings and even deliver them for a while.

After you understand what works and what doesn't at a smaller scale, you start the delegation process assuming things will keep working like they were when you were delivering, until they don't.

And here you are, being pulled into the weeds again and again. We don't want that for you because the goal of building a team is to give you the freedom you want.

Even if you don't have a fulfillment team delivering your service, you want the process to be streamlined to get you out of the weeds.

You need an Ideal Customer Engineer or several on your team. I like to use the abbreviation ICE for Ideal Customer Engineer . You can be warm with clients, but mentally you're methodical and cold as ICE: be pragmatic and helpful, and guide them to where they want and need to be.

This book will give you the frameworks you need to train your team or yourself to stop being an Account Manager, Coach, or Accountability buddy, in order to become an Ideal Customer Engineer.

This new role will make your marketing efforts deflationary and it will also help make any client transform from not-a-great-fit to an ideal client.

Before I go into the details on what and where this Ideal Customer Engineer should be focused, I want you to keep a couple of skills in mind that will help the right person become the Ideal Customer Engineer in less than 30 days. To step into this new role, they need to:

- Be Organized.

- Be Detail-oriented.

- Be Good at time management and follow-through.

- Know behavioral approaches and how to sell the process (through habit change).

- Understand Persuasion/influence/negotiation techniques (speaking and writing for different communication channels).

- Ask good questions (motivational interviewing and probing).

- Have Process flexibility (meet clients where they are).

- Be Grounded and realistic.

Keep in mind now that when you have this new role of the Ideal Customer Engineer, the main goal is for them to be the trusted Guide for your clients. Imagine this person being the Go-To Person, a real Mentor for your clients.

When I think about mentorship, I think about someone who focuses on improvement and helping their clients push further and closer to the life they want. In the book *The Power of Moments*, the Heath brothers came up with a great definition of what mentorship should look like:

- Expectations on the Ideal Customer Engineer's end = High Standards + Assurance

- Mentorship = Direction + Support

So for a great customer experience and mentorship, we should keep standards high for our clients while providing them with assurance, direction, and support. It's like saying:

"I have expectations for you, and I know you can meet them. So try this new challenge, and I'll help you recover if you fail."

You'll see later on how much this can help when dealing with specific subgroups of clients. This approach will help your clients increase self-confidence, trust the process, and take more action.

This is how you create a connection with their Aspirational Identity, create more buy-in, and escalate their commitment. But none of these should be interpreted as an opportunity to save clients. It's quite the opposite.

Donald Miller wrote a fantastic book, *Building a Storybrand*, which is a great interpretation of how you should see your or your team's new role.

In your Customer's Journey, your fulfillment team's primary role is to be the Guide. Why? Because that's the mentorship process clients need to go through to reach their goals, the goal is not to save clients; the goal is for them to feel like the real heroes of their story.

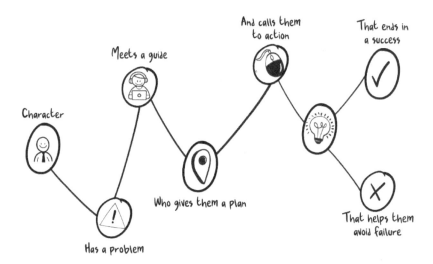

Your goal, now that the client knows they have a problem and realize they need your help to solve it, is to be their Guide. As a Guide, you'll give them a plan, and it will get them into action. That plan not only helps them achieve the outcomes they want, but it will also keep them from failing.

The analogy used in *Building a Storybrand* is the *Movie Hunger Games,* where Katniss Everdeen volunteers to play in Hunger Games, where the participants will fight to the death. She is unprepared to face this problem alone, so she meets Haymitch, who will be her guide and the one who calls her to action.

The Ideal Customer Engineer is Haymitch, your client Katniss, and this is the journey. I hope not as life and death as Hunger Games, but almost as exciting!

This process of being a Guide will help build something life-changing for your clients: the untapped power of <u>courage</u>.

When I talk about courage, it's not the absence of fear. It is the mastery of dealing with anxiety and moments of tension. When you guide your clients to be the hero they were meant to be, they'll be proud of themselves, see the barriers they have overcome, look back at all the victories won, and see how success was earned.

Now that you have some of the fundamentals lined up, are you ready for the fulfillment continuum?

What is Fulfillment, btw?

Fulfillment is an interesting word, so let's make sure you understand what I mean when I use the word fulfillment moving forward.

Fulfillment:

1. the achievement of something desired, promised, or predicted.

"Winning the championship was the fulfillment of a childhood dream."

2. the meeting of a requirement, condition, or need.

"The fulfillment of statutory requirements"

We're not talking about personal fulfillment. We're talking here about how you can meet your customer's needs, generally associated with the big promise that attracted them to hire you.

Fulfillment is present at different stages of your customer journey, including but not limited to:

- Handoff from sales to service delivery.

- Welcoming and onboarding clients to start benefiting from the service.

- Keep clients on track for the end goal.

- Delivery and meeting expectations.

- Understanding what the customer needs after the first goal, and continuing to work with the customer for longer.

For that to happen, we need some key ingredients, which will be thoroughly covered in this chapter and the following ones.

To create a great experience and deliver with consistency and predictability, your clients need to move across what we call the Fulfillment Continuum.

If I could describe this in layman's terms, your goal with fulfillment and moving clients across the continuum is to get them from "unsure" to "let's do it." This will help your clients take action and to be completely bought in, based on the new belief you have instilled in their mindset. You need that piece as part of your customer's journey because all actions are belief-driven.

The Fulfillment Continuum

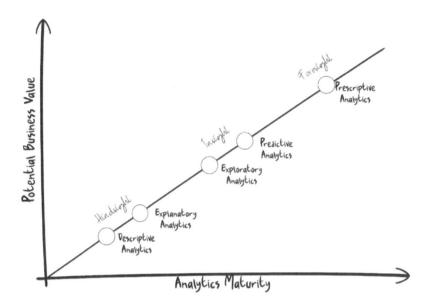

What is a continuum? I'll keep this one short, but have a look at the picture above.

The Fulfillment Continuum is when you gather hindsight, insight, and foresight together to improve someone's situation. It could be for a client working with you or even for yourself on how to make your business better.

When you think about a continuum, you want to understand the following:

- **Hindsight**

    o   What happened?

    o   Why is this happening?

- **Insight**

  - What's the reason for this happening?

  - What will happen now?

- **Foresight**

  - How can you make this happen? Or how can you avoid this happening again?

Let's break down what I mean by the fulfillment continuum and how the previous concepts apply. This might sound different from anything you've heard or read, but psychology is key to really understanding your business and customers. I'll give you a bit more context.

I fell in love with psychology, sociology, and behavioral economics long ago when trying to discover myself and to understand my flaws as a human being. In that process, I became equipped with many tools, ideas, and frameworks that were easily applied to my service-based business and has worked like a charm for other online service-based companies.

So when we launched our Consulting offer, I applied this analysis with businesses that weren't profitable or that were struggling to cross the chasm:

- What is happening in the business?

  - Most were less and less profitable over time.

- Why is this happening?

    - Little to no retention, drop-offs, and refunds.

- What's the reason this is happening?

    - The journey wouldn't allow for Relationships at Scale.

- What will happen now?

    - The business can easily become obsolete if this is not addressed.

- How can we make this happen?

    - Implementing psychological solutions that address the customer journey for a great experience and increase client engagement.

This gave birth to our focus when working with our Consulting Clients, all based on a simple analysis. We came up with some standard metrics that we focus on, like getting our consulting clients a 50-80% success rate. This is what you want from an offer that has applied what was covered in the High LTV offer chapter. If you haven't gone through the exercise to review your offer ingredients, you can pause and go through it before we focus on the tactical pieces.

Notice how we focused on 50-80%. It's unrealistic to try to aim for 100% of your clients being successful because in any offer, whether it is Done For You (DFY), Done with You (DWY), or Do It Yourself (DIY), there are the elements of life, randomness, and other issues out of the scope of the offer that can keep people from getting what they want.

In an industry like the online service-based market, specifically, the high ticket one, where you see numbers like a 5-15% success rate, 50-80% is solid, healthy, and ethical.

So when you think about the Fulfillment Continuum, this is what you want to picture in your mind:

Regret $\longleftarrow$ $\longrightarrow$ Engaged
Buyer's Remorse Buy-in

Buy-in and Buyer's Remorse

If you think about your service, there are two extremes your clients could be: either they're full of buyer's remorse, or they're entirely bought in. And why do I call it a continuum? Because it's not binary, that would assume clients will just be a 0 or a 1. But this is an ongoing process, not a single event.

The Fulfillment Continuum is a process, so clients can go from one side of the continuum to the other while using your service and progressing, regressing, or staying in the same phase for a time.

Let me break down the concept so you understand precisely what this means. Buyer's remorse, quite simply, means they have feelings of regret about the decision they made.

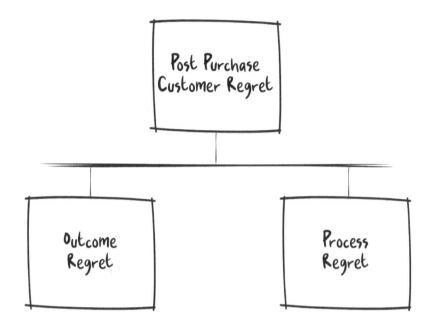

We're talking about people regretting what they bought, which can be broken down into two different categories:

1. Outcome regret

   a. Regret due to other alternatives; this could be reflected in the high LTV offer ingredient, Perceived Likelihood of Achievement, and can damage the perceived value.

   b. Regret due to change in significance, and this can be reflected in the high LTV offer ingredient, Big Outcome, and can damage the perceived value.

2. Process regret

    a. Regret due to the lack of consideration of the process. This could be reflected in the high LTV offer ingredient, Effort, and can damage the perceived value.

    b. Regret due to the consideration of the process. This can be reflected in the high LTV offer ingredient, Time Delay, and can damage the perceived value.

For a simpler term, I will call this feeling of regret, Buyer's remorse, and it's the extreme opposite of Buy-in. Let's check the meaning of the two according to Wikipedia.

Buyer's remorse

1. a feeling of regret experienced after making a purchase, typically one regarded as unnecessary or extravagant.

"the winning bidder might well have a case of buyer's remorse."

Buy-in

1. acceptance of and willingness to actively support and participate in something (such as a proposed new plan or policy)

"without buy-in from his players, Gruden's just another tuned-out coach."

You have a good idea now of what those two concepts mean, but how can you understand where your clients are or should be in different parts of their journey? Where are your clients in that continuum?

Let's go through some examples of how Ben and I have seen this work. Both for our businesses in the past and for almost all of our Consulting clients.

Starting with buy-in, how can you get more clients to be bought in and benefit from your offerings? A simple answer would be you need to get your clients in action.

But the obvious statement above doesn't address the reality, which is that your clients are not getting into action. And when you look at your active client list, you can see they're not committed.

That commitment you want can be engineered, and that's your next step. Why are your clients not committed and stuck in this Buyer's Remorse stage? Why are they not moving forward and completely bought in?

Escalation of Commitment

When someone purchases something or invests in something but they understand things won't be as magical as promised, they face a dilemma and a possible feeling of regret:

- Should I pull out all my resources and invest more in an

alternative solution that can give me a similar outcome, or should I stick to my initial decision and hope this will pay off long-term?

- o You will see this when clients want to drop out or ask for a refund, mainly because they've been targeted by another offer that promised a similar outcome, but it's just shiny object syndrome.

If they were committed, they wouldn't be second-guessing everything, and this is why getting them to move from left to right on the continuum is a must. We want an escalation of commitment.

Escalation of commitment is a risk whenever someone commits resources to a course of action to achieve a positive outcome and experiences disappointing results. Invested resources can take any form, from time, money, and labor to mental and emotional energy.

I know this can feel a bit technical, but I will make sure to break this down in simple layperson's terms. Your client not only takes risks when they purchase your offer, but they'll be taking further risks by investing their time and effort to make it work for them. That can cause doubt for them, and if you understand that, you can adjust the delivery and communication style to prevent those feelings. Accept that, and you can use your understanding of psychology to help them.

When your clients are stuck in their minds, experiencing indecision, you have one of the most valuable opportunities during the customer journey. Your clients have the opportunity to escalate their commitment. This will be easy to spot around the main inflection points of your offer.

But that decision to be more committed depends on a lot of things, and sometimes it's not obvious. In the next picture, you can see some of their thoughts, values, and beliefs that can help them to escalate their commitment:

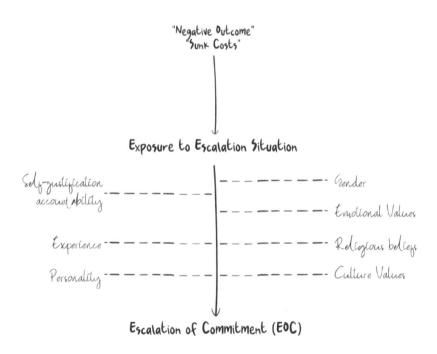

We want them to escalate their commitment because this will use three of the most significant human biases:

- **Loss aversion**. When customers receive feedback that their investment is failing, they are faced with the idea of losing both the potential rewards the investment initially offered and the resources previously committed to it.

  ○ For example, the pain of losing $1,000 is more extreme than the pleasure of gaining $1,000. This loss framing may lead clients to go to great lengths and take unwise risks to avoid losses.

- **Sunk costs**. The more resources spent on an investment, the more likely a client will escalate commitment. However, because these resources are irrecoverable, it is irrational to factor them into decisions about future outcomes. The desire to honor sunk costs is driven by psychological factors, including loss aversion (refusing to accept the "loss" of expended resources), self-justification (needing to justify past expenditures to oneself), and impression management (wanting to avoid appearing wasteful to others).

  ○ For example, when someone is in a toxic relationship and has invested so much energy. Even though they know there is no bright future, they keep investing, expecting some magic to happen.

- **Proximity to completion**. The closer a project is to fruition, the more likely customers will embody escalation of commitment. Invested time is one form of sunk cost, so it is more difficult to abandon a project the nearer it comes to completion. Because customers become caught up in the desire to finish the project, they are more likely to escalate their commitment to realizing their goals even when other, more attractive alternatives are available.

You can use the psychology described to make them so invested in the offer that the pain of losing the money invested and the effort applied is more painful than starting a new offer with a competitor or the pain of just quitting and calling it a day.

There are many reasons why people don't take action when they want to improve their lives. Fear, regret, and uncertainty can all keep us from moving forward and away from buy-in. Luckily, there's a way to overcome these barriers. The process of overcoming them starts with taking small steps and believing in yourself and your ability to overcome any obstacle you face.

This will be the relationship between perceived risk and perceived responsibility, as depicted in the picture below:

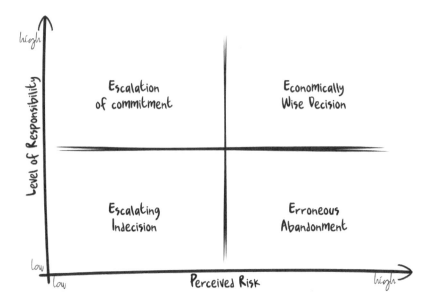

When you look at that picture, your goal is for your clients to stay in the Escalation of commitment zone: demonstrating high levels of responsibility with low perceived risk.

Yes, there will be moments when the stakes are high. Your clients might quit if they feel like they are responsible for the outcomes, but the risk is so high that they're better off just leaving. The goal would be to reduce the perceived threat, so they feel like they are in the commitment zone. This is why the concept of Relationships at Scale is so brilliant. Relationships at Scale allow them to stay in the commitment zone.

Another situation you'll face is that some clients start to ghost you within the first couple of weeks of working together, this Erroneous Abandonment is based on a high perceived risk with a shallow level of responsibility on their end. You'll find later in the book that some archetypes are more prone to that than others.

The fourth scenario you will see is when a client starts working with you and feels a deficient level of responsibility, but because the stakes are low, they're unsure what to do. The worst thing you can do here is increase the perception of risk because that'll lead to abandonment.

Long story short, the goal is to get someone who is unsure about the risk of working with you, to be fully committed, and to take the appropriate steps to be successful. This is the perfect tie-in of the principal elements of the High LTV offer: You get them to walk towards their Big Outcome while making the Belief real, which will drive their actions and propel them forward.

Before we move on, I want to go through a relaxing exercise. I know some of your pains because I've been there, but I also know how easy it is to think that everything is bad and broken.

But it isn't.

Negative bias and Fulfillment Energy Expenditure

It's easy to get caught up in what's not working, which we already addressed, but our goal is to expand the experience, not to narrow it.

After understanding what we have covered, most businesses go into reactive mode and try to save or recover everyone who is disappointed with what they purchased. But do you remember I said your goal was to get 50-80% of clients to have success in working with you?

My goal was to point out a negative bias that messes up your focus and action. To build a highly profitable business with excellent retention and LTV, you need to refine your focus. Let's see why and how.

You get 10 emails, 9 give incredible feedback, and 1 gives negative feedback. You remember the negative one.

You get 10 excellent reviews and 1 bad one... and you can't sleep thinking about the bad one.

Remember that you're in the human-to-human business, so owners, teams, and customers all suffer from the same biases and heuristics. And we are all wired to focus on negative signals. Me, Ben, and you.

Although this all sounds like common sense, it's not common practice. Having inflection points in your offer is okay and can actually be good for you and for your clients. It can create excitement and focus; this is why you need to have Peaks and Valleys in your customer journey.

What we've seen in most service-based businesses is a mix of neutral moments and small Valleys, at best.

And the business owner focuses like crazy on filling the valleys and maybe later builds some peaks if the customer is lucky. That's too much focus on the negative, an exaggeration of focus on the Buyer's remorse stage.

What feels more urgent to you? Fixing a client deliverable that is not working or sending a physical gift to a client who had a major win and breakthrough?

There is no perfect answer here, but heuristics and biases will get the best of you. As a business owner, you want a complaint-free business, which I appreciate. And yes, when consulting with a client, we focus on how to make their fulfillment smooth without creating any significant valleys, but we don't focus on perfection. Because a Raving Fan business is about meeting clients' expectations, not necessarily exceeding them.

Let's do an exercise. This will show you how being deliberate with the implementation of these concepts can and should be.

What if you gave all of your customers a survey to rate the service you provided on a scale from 1-7:

- Where 1 is deplorable service.

- 4 is neutral service.

- 7 is a perfect service.

Who would you focus on? Imagine I present you with two options:

- Plan A focuses on bringing the 1,2,3 (negatives) to a neutral state (4).

- Plan B focuses on bringing the 4,5,6 (positives) to a max elevation (7).

Which plan would you choose? A or B? Before you say "both," you know energy is finite, and you know that those who try to catch two rabbits simultaneously catch none. So which one would you go with?

Almost every business we have worked with focuses 80% on Plan A (recovering unhappy customers) and 20% of their time on Plan B (getting good clients to become great). It kind of sounds logical, right?

But it's not. This is a human bias, a real trap. And this has been studied, analyzed, and detailed in several surveys, including the 2016 Survey: The US customer Experience index by researchers at Forrester.

They went through this exercise and compared the difference in revenue generated after implementing both Plan A and Plan B.

What's the difference between people in "group A" versus people in "group B"?

The results were staggering. Ordinary people who rate a service-based business a 7 (very good) spend 2-3x more money than a 4 (neutral). And much more than that when we compare a client who rates your service a 7 versus someone who rates it a 1, 2, or 3 (negative).

It makes sense, you know that happy people spend more money. So if happy people spend more, what can you conclude?

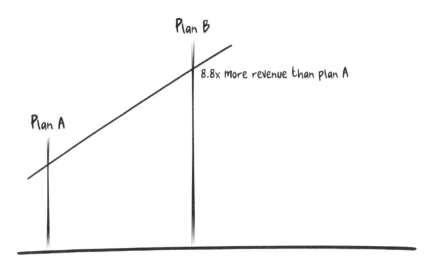

A transition from a client that's a 4 (neutral) to a 7 (very good) generates more money than a client that's a 1 (very bad) to a 4 (neutral). Although the effort in implementing the action plans is similar.

And if you look back at your business, if it's running with some congruency for a while, you'll have more people in the 4-6 group (positive) than the 1-3 group (negative).

So for the same level of effort, you have a lot more value per person, focusing on taking the good to great. Can you see how your brain and its biases can screw up your efforts?

You're wired to focus on the negative. That's a fast way to lose money, or at least not spend it wisely. Plan B can generate close to nine times more capital than Plan A. Please reread it: almost 9 times more. The remainder of this book is focused on preventing those valleys but much more focused on accelerating all the neutral customers into raving fan customers. This is how your LTV will skyrocket faster than you ever imagined.

Caveat: we still believe you should optimize all the valleys, but between pleasing a client who doesn't like the "green color" you used in your slide deck and sending a warm voice message to a client who's doing well, the latter can pay you 9x more for the same effort.

PS: We didn't consider extra revenue. Once you get people to spend more with you, they usually refer more people to work with you. Double win.

Keep calm, my friend; going all in can also bring some diminishing returns.

The law of Diminishing Returns

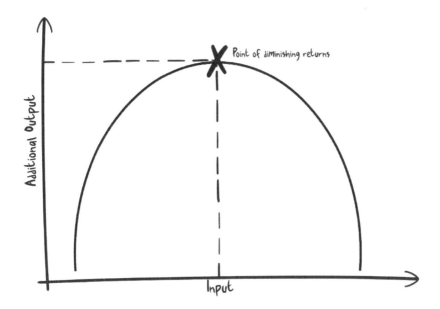

I want to start with a word of advice: most businesses want to do everything while looking for the pinnacle of success. But I know that's not sustainable nor needed, like the example about exceeding versus meeting expectations. This is because your efforts follow an inverted U distribution model.

This simple concept from the fundamentals of the productivity economy is the law of diminishing returns.

This has been popularized by many concepts, including Nassim Taleb's Concavity effects.

The concept is quite simple: for every unit of input, you get less and less additional output. Eventually you reach the point of diminishing returns, which not only doesn't add any result, it can also introduce losses.

Let's think about a simple example, like fat loss. If you have a couple of pounds to lose and you're doing nothing, adding the habit of daily walks and focusing on drinking more water will immediately help you see some results.

Input: water and walking

Output: better mood and maybe a little weight loss

If you decide to keep adding inputs, like tracking your calories, you'll see some additional improvements. Then, later you might choose to add strength training, and you'll see some more progress but not as noticeable as before.

As you keep improving and adding stuff, you get less of a return, and people tend to fall prey to adding more to keep the machine running at full speed at the expense of crossing the point of diminishing returns.

The same logic applies to rebuilding your customer success approach after going through this book. Using one to three ideas for your business will create immediate results with sound output, but if you decide to do it all at once, you will risk crossing the point of diminishing returns and doing more harm than good.

So your goal is not for you to use all the magic in this book and make the customer service process more complex than it needs to be. The goal is to make it good. Because if you feel like it's not where you want it to be, something needs to change.

No business can be great with terrible service.

But when you reach an acceptable level of quality, the things that make the offer great are tangential to the big primary outcome. It's not easy to promise more, but making it more enjoyable is always okay. So the touchpoints you have planned with clients, the communications style you'll learn in this book, and the baseline for a profitable business will be easier, faster, and more reliable than just stacking more.

Sorry for interrupting the flow, but I know how easy it is to get overly excited and then want to do too much, too fast. Now that you know we want to be great but that there are some diminishing returns, let's look at what clients really want...

Sell them what they want, give them what they need, bro

This is the biggest mismatch for a Customer Success focused company's message. Picture this: you enter Mcdonald's and ask for a burger.

They think you're fat. They give you a salad. How would you feel?

I would feel disappointed. And that could be happening to your clients also.

So it's not about giving your clients what they need. That's not how you get buy-in.

They want what they want, and if you don't understand that, expectations can become impossible to meet. When you don't meet expectations, they end up not meeting their goals, losing belief that the goal is attainable for them, which creates a high perception of effort, adding more time needed to hit their target, and they'll get close to zero perceived value from your offer.

Do you see how these concepts are all interconnected?

If your company's experience doesn't feel cohesive, clients will become confused and disappointed. It's like going to a Michelin 5-star restaurant with a great Chef to find the place is a mess, stinks, and has an awful ambiance. You regret going there, even though the food was supposedly great.

Like the restaurant, you want to address both sides of the equation and give clients the product they think they paid for, but we will create a context in which they can truly benefit and enjoy the product. The buy-in process helps create that context for enjoyment.

And the buy-in process, or avoidance of buyer's remorse, starts during the sales process. A good sales process, either on the phone, in person, or through a sales page, stretches the gap between your client's actual starting point and their Big Outcome.

It could even make them feel bad about where they are now, but at the same time, when we overpromise during the sales process, this makes clients believe they can achieve more than what they actually can in a short time frame. Clients love it, speed to results and Big Outcome? That's a high perceived value for that offer. They're sold.

But if the process they need to follow is barely mentioned during that sales process, and you understand why that would be the case because you want to avoid prospects being overly logical or using too many facts and numbers, but that sets you and your clients up for disappointment and failure. That's how marketing and sales generally work, but not fulfillment and customer success.

As the Customer Success team, your goal is to address those known patterns and faulty thoughts as early as possible to make clients move along the continuum.

Fulfillment must bridge the gap between sales, the Big Outcome, high expectations, and how you can deliver all of that. To become a one-of-a-kind, star business, an exponential S-curve kind of business that crosses the chasm with success and builds relationships at scale, you need to make Buy-in your first goal.

The Buy-in starts when clients escalate their commitment after being sold on the process. Those small tiny behaviors help your clients implement the steps needed to get closer to the Big Outcome. That's when magic creates real and amazing outcomes.

Buy-in Framework

There are three things to know about building a solid Buy-in process:

- What looks like a people problem is often a situation problem.

- What looks like laziness is often exhaustion.

- What looks like resistance is often a lack of clarity.

So instead of thinking everything is broken, that you have the wrong clients, or that this offer can't scale, let's contextualize.

People get excited quickly by a new promise, even if the outcome is not known. Marketers nailed this long ago, and this is how markets work.

What you want is a story about your business that sells. An immeasurable aspect of fulfillment is that it will enable you to tell a story and build a narrative around your brand. This is almost impossible to measure, but that narrative helps anchor higher prices for the offer the customer purchased and other offers they might buy.

The cycle will be transformative for you because the fulfillment funnel builds loyalty and creates trust, customers keep sharing the narrative with others, and you will be even more trustworthy. The first step is to implement the buy-in framework to create the momentum your clients need.

The Buy-in implementation can help you do what's pictured:

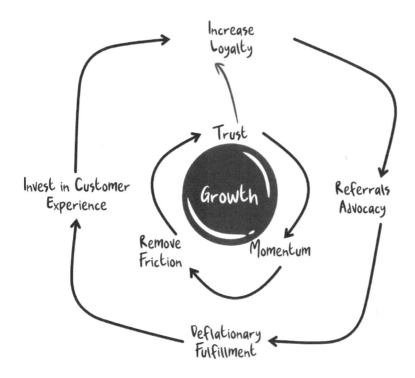

Your main goal is to create a Deflationary Fulfillment department that gets cheaper and cheaper over time, so for every unit of effort, you can get a better ROI without compromising on quality.

This is why, as depicted in the image above, the growth goes from the inside out. You start with an excellent customer experience that creates trust and momentum. You focus on removing friction, which continues to increase confidence and momentum.

After the first cycle is built, you create a parallel flywheel: you increase loyalty which will increase advocacy like referrals and word of mouth, which leads to deflationary fulfillment as you're getting more clients and LTV spending the same amount of money to acquire customers as you were before, but getting more clients. This leads to more money to invest in Customer Experience, accelerating this process over and over again.

You need to remember that what works for one part of the business might not work for others, and this is where this book comes to life, to help you with the coaching and delivery processes that are different from marketing and sales. Let's focus on the internal part of the flywheel, which is to create Trust and Momentum, what we call Buy-in.

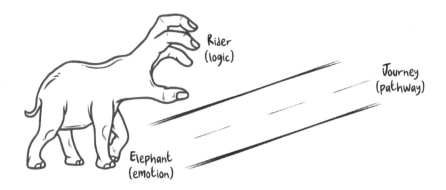

144

As a customer success person and Ideal Customer Engineer, your goal is to embody Buy-in in everything you do to move people across the continuum. The Happiness Hypothesis book introduced me to a great concept called The Elephant and the Rider.

This concept describes how you can observe the human mind. The Rider represents reason that tries its best to direct an emotional and stubborn Elephant. But the Elephant is typically the more powerful force, stubborn, and has its own will. It will only comply with the Rider's commands if those commands do not conflict with its desires. The Elephant is always looking for a quick reward and not any long-term benefits.

How often have you instructed your Rider to go on a diet to become healthier and live a more vibrant life, only to find your Elephant eating a cupcake?

You can't just convince clients, you need them to be bought in: they need direction, an elephant that's rewarded with some peanuts, and a way to keep them on an easy path.

This concept has been popularized through many different analogies and books:

- The chimp and the human, in the Chimp Paradox.

- The fast brain and the slow brain, in Thinking Fast and Slow.

I'll stick with the elephant because they're nice and tall like Ben and me.

All these books and analogies describe a simple fact: our mind is in a constant battle when making decisions, even the small ones. You've probably heard or used some of these expressions:

- Head vs. gut.

- Left vs. right brain.

- Frontal cortex vs. limbic system.

- Conscious vs. unconscious.

- Old brain vs. new brain.

Let's bring this framework to life so that regardless of how the customer is wired, you know exactly what will help them take action and be more committed.

Buy-in can be broken down into a three-part framework:

- The Emotion, which is the Elephant.

- The Logic, which is the Rider.

- The Pathway, which is the Journey ahead of them.

So, to get Buy-in, we need to direct The Rider, motivate The Elephant, and shape The Pathway. This interesting and useful framework comes from the book The Switch.

When thinking about the Rider, some people might look like they have a Rider that is super resistant, which is often a sign of lack of clarity. If the Rider has no crystal-clear direction, it will be hard to convince him to take on the workload. We will explore how to do this in detail in the application chapter going through ideas for your clients like the welcome process, onboarding, support, and tracking.

If the Rider is convinced, now you need to motivate the Elephant. When dealing with a customer that looks lazy, they're typically just exhausted. So although you have convinced the Rider where he should go, he can't use force successfully for very long before the Elephant wins. It's essential to engage your customer's emotional side to get them to be cooperative and motivated to act. When you uncover the meaning behind their Big Outcome, mark the milestones and explain how things connect, you have a much more motivated Elephant. This can be covered in almost any interaction with customers, but if you do any form of onboarding, usually this is the best starting point to understand and motivate their Elephant.

Finally, you need a map for a laser-focused Rider and motivated Elephant. When you Shape the Pathway, and your customers know where they're going, you recontextualize everything.

Here is something to think about, what looks like a people problem is often a situation problem, so when you recontextualize it with a new pathway that you control, you change the environment to a richer one. This will make behavior change and Buy-in more likely, no matter what's happening with the Rider or the Elephant.

I know it can feel like a lot, but you'll see these concepts overlapping in almost every chapter in this book which will help it make sense and also easy to apply to your Fulfillment Funnel. Things change when you keep buy-in as your goal. Understand that it's not an event like a sale, but more like a process. We will go into the how of all of this in the fulfillment clinic later in the chapter.

Remember that for clients to go through a successful change, it requires a translation of ambiguous goals or Aspirational Identity into concrete behaviors. You must tell them about the next critical moves to get clients bought in. What about their own will and expectations?

Expectation management

Expectations shape our reality. Our expectations about what will happen can influence what happens, so this is critical when working with clients. There is a domino-like process when managing expectations well:

- Our beliefs change emotions and create positive

expectations

- Our beliefs redirect attention, and what we focus on tends to expand

- Our beliefs change motivation and help us to be more deliberate

- Our beliefs affect physiology; a good example is how a placebo works in the body.

So if you want to shape your client's experience, you need to help them manage their emotions, attention, motivation, and physiology. Also, this is another reason why buy-in and honing in on this framework will completely change how your business operates as a whole.

Expectations = Time x Effort

We have talked about clients' expectations, but we never said what it means. Basically, expectations are the result of the bottom part of the High LTV offer equation.

Are you starting to see how everything I'm sharing aligns?

Whenever you work with someone that has high expectations, they think it is a result of the top part of the high LTV offer equation. The customer feels that their expectation is their Big

Outcome multiplied by them Believing it.

That's not the reality. That's the marketing angle. The fulfillment angle explains to the customer that their expectation results from their effort multiplied by the amount of time they do it.

Suppose your client has great expectations about your offer. In that case, it's your role as a Customer Success team to explain what timeline and effort are expected from them as a customer to make that expectation a reality.

Understanding the mechanisms behind expectations is critical for the goal of creating Relationships at Scale, and the two main variables are:

1. Belief

    - When we believe something is possible, we put in the effort and embrace a timeline. And when someone cares about us and treats us well, we're more likely to have the belief and thus a positive outcome.

2. Conditioning

    - Like Pavlov's dogs, our body builds expectancy after repeated experiences and releases various chemicals to prepare us for the future.

You need to help them connect the dots and have realistic

expectations, which opens a conversation that helps you navigate their reality more constructively. You can understand what they believe and how they have been conditioned.

When you clarify what the sales process meant by the Big Outcome, and you go through what effort is needed to make the expectation a reality within your program timeline, you start a compelling conversation with your customers:

- If they can't put in all that effort, they need to be open to negotiating the outcome or the timeline, e.g.:

    o With effort, I would frame it not as the quantity but the quality of work they need to put in to see results and even frame it as an average of how many hours a day and week they need to make it happen.

    o For our consulting clients, 1-2 hours a week will get them results, and we explain that during our sales process to ensure they know what they need to understand to know if they're ready to work with us.

- Suppose your client is bought into getting the results within the timeline. In that case, you need to find ways to make their efforts match what is required, and thus tracking their behaviors, leading indicators, and lag indicators will be essential (I'll share more in the Bonus Section).

- If clients are open to negotiating the timeline and effort, you can now manage the new expectation and hold them accountable.

  - If they're okay with extending timelines, you planted your first seed for at least a continuation offer that will keep them working with you for a while; thus, you get a healthy extension of contracts.

What you're doing is allowing your clients to choose their own pace and manage their expectations. You don't want the customer to try to do it within your timeline. That's one of the reasons they'll blame you for not meeting their expectations. You want to hold them accountable for their decision of how long it will take.

It's like playing a video game. By default, you go with the Intermediate level, but you can always ask them what difficulty level they want.

Although this approach generally covers human psychology, does this work for every customer the same way? No, it won't. This is why I said you want Relationships at Scale.

And those relationships will shape the whole experience, as it will affect how you're connecting with them, how magical the experience you're creating is, and how psychology plays for or against you. Using the concepts we've discussed so far will create one of the most potent sources of energy and motivation for humans: anticipation.

I'll use this survey as an example of how perceptions are crucial to customer success:

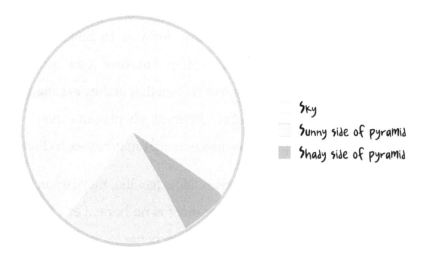

Get what I'm saying? You thought I would present you with great numbers and figures, and you can now see only a pyramid. Our brain is magical.

Think about your everyday Relationships before you think about them at scale. When you schedule something with people you like, you get so excited about the day to come! That energy is aligned with your non-linear perception of time (I covered that in the Time Delay sub-chapter).

That excitement can make the perception of time change and be used to create even more buy-in. But remember, anticipation is not necessarily a good or bad thing. It will always depend on what clients are looking for. If you can make your clients excited, it's a good kind of energy. If you make them overly anxious, it will backfire and not help them take action.

You have so much more power now to not only help your clients, but to also help yourself. It's time for you to integrate the fulfillment continuum into your offer, but first, you need to understand who your client is. We will do that in the next chapter by explaining how to bucket different clients and how to implement the concepts above in a way that matches each client.

The only exception is when those clients feel like they're stuck at the bottom, the ones that feel like there is no hope. Let's look at how to understand them and serve them better.

Learned hopelessness

Before starting a journey with a client, you need to understand what they have in mind. One of the books I like the most that shares an interesting concept on this is called the *Happiness Advantage*.

In the book, the author talks about Principle #4, which can help us to be more positive and willing to fail and can put us on a path to success in life. It can also help you get the thing you want the most from your clients, buy-in.

And when you go back to the fulfillment continuum, you can see that your client's mindset can change across the continuum. They'll have more skepticism and a glass half-empty mentality when they're close to the buyer's remorse side, but a glass half-full mentality when they're entirely bought in.

He shares a study that has, in my opinion, one of the most exciting behavioral ideas. The American psychologist Martin Seligman researched and analyzed learned hopelessness.

He was interested in understanding depression, which triggered him to follow his passion and learn more about human behavior. The study I'm going to highlight was conducted on dogs, but it also translates perfectly in humans.

Learned Hopelessness

They took three groups of dogs and placed them in a cage.

Group 1 was placed in a harness for a time just to be released later.

Groups 2 and 3 were different, and these dogs were given shocks at random times. The difference between groups 2 and 3 is that dogs from group 2 had a lever they could press to stop the shocks.

Group 3 suffered because they had no control over how to stop the shocks.

The exciting part of this experiment was when they moved the dogs to a chamber with two rectangular compartments divided by a barrier a few inches high.

All the dogs could escape the shocks on one side of the box by jumping to the other side.

The dogs in groups 1 and 2 quickly learned this task and escaped the shock.

Most group 3 dogs, that had previously learned that nothing they did would affect the shock, laid down passively and suffered while being shocked.

The dogs in group 3 learned hopelessness. And I'm not saying your clients are dogs, but they could be suffering from the same thing, and it's keeping them stuck at the low end of the continuum.

Some clients have a big problem in life, learned hopelessness, and then stop even bothering to try.

If you help them to take action by implementing what we're teaching you, you're not only creating a great client, but this will also carry over to other areas of their life. You could be changing someone's life forever with your offer, and there is no way someone won't become a Raving Fan after that.

Moving people from left to right in the continuum is a great exercise that helps them look at all problems as opportunities to uncover who they can become on the other side.

Understanding motivation

Getting clients to understand motivation and how short-term efforts create long-term results is one of the most important things when managing them.

There are no wasted efforts. There is work being accomplished. But there are also non-evident results from that work.

An example of this is when you have an ice cube. Imagine it's at 25° and in solid form. Suddenly you start to warm the ice cube, but it remains rock solid.

Out of the blue, when the temperature reaches 32°, the ice cube melts and becomes water!

Was it magic? No.

The melting process was happening, but it couldn't be seen until it crossed the tipping point. And the same applies to you and to your client's results.

I love this graph created by James Clear. Showing what clients think will happen and what happens in reality:

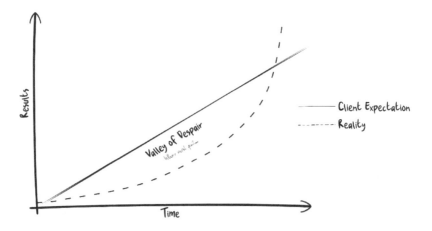

Most people think results will be linear, and when they understand they're not, because we're building the foundations, they get stuck in what he calls the Valley of Despair. And this affects me, you and your clients.

They're dropping off or leaving at a point where if they crossed that tipping point, the results wouldn't be linear; the results would be exponential. The only way you have to shift your clients' mindset is to manage expectations.

Their motivation will correlate to everything we talked about so far, Emotional Buy-in, expectation management, clear communication, the identity they want to build, and the trust in you.

Imagine you ask someone to cross a bridge that is on the ground. Would they do it? Probably.

What if that bridge was not on the floor but between two buildings? Will they still do it? Most people probably wouldn't.

But what if you pay them 1 million dollars? Would they do it? Some yes, some no. But their motivation has already changed.

Another option is that you decide not to give them 1 million dollars, but the building they're in now is on fire. Would they cross the bridge to run away from the fire? Oh yes, they would, and I think we all would.

Motivation is contextual, and we can change the context when we feel clients don't have it. In the example above, you went from someone not being willing to cross a bridge across two buildings, even if you paid them 1 million dollars, to suddenly getting them to cross for free. Interesting right?

Let's go one layer deeper. Now the fire is not on your side but on the other side. Would you cross it? Probably not, even if you were paid a million dollars, because it doesn't make sense.

Unless, in the other building, there was a loved one, a child, would you cross the bridge?

Most people would say yes to the latter without monetary incentives or cost-benefit analysis. Based on their identity, it is the only choice that makes sense. This is why understanding the Big Outcome and Aspirational Identity is crucial.

Whenever you work with clients, you need to know who they want to be. You can help them explore the options available to reach that destination and find an action plan to start immediately.

You also need to remember that results take time, and there will be times when the work looks like it's a waste of time and effort, but it's not. This will lead to ups and downs in client motivation, you will face a very stubborn Elephant, and you need to know how to avoid this trap.

Remember that Motivation is contextual, and as Ideal Customer Engineers, we can help change the context.

You can engineer success to create hope and motivation that is the best fuel for clients who struggle with taking action. This increases their belief as well while also increasing motivation and buy-in.

But before you go all in, let's see it in practice.

Fulfillment Continuum Clinic

From a client of ours:

"Just wanted to pop in here to say happy Friday to y'all and to report that the most recent report from this September morning shows that our "success rate" (essentially our "course completion rate") is at 83.33% this month for the program in which we as a team have been studiously implementing the raving fan formula and this month 5/6 have successfully launched! That was under a 20% success rate back in June.

Lots of factors at play here, one of which is selling to a better avatar. But I think one big factor has been our welcome/onboarding/syncing with the sales team to have better communication in the way you guys prescribe, and I'm very pleased with the path we're on. Can't wait to move the needle even further with hopefully more volume, some kind of recurring revenue/retention strategy, and of course, developing a referral system. Woohoo!"

This company is not suffering from the Sisyphus Tale anymore. They figured out how Buy–in works and how helping clients take action is transformative at all levels for a service-based business.

And we've seen this many times. After spending time with more than 100 businesses, we've seen this working with all the different niches you can think of:

- Coaches

- Consultants

- Digital Agencies

- Authors

- Saas products

- Ecommerce

- Brick and mortar

- Startup Incubators

It always works because it's the psychology of how humans work. It doesn't matter what type of business you have. If you are dealing with humans, having coaching skills will make your life easier by getting quicker buy-in, increasing client confidence, and getting clients results faster through a better understanding. Finally, this brings us to the secret sauce: Raving Fans.

This is why I started with the concept of the Ideal Customer Engineer; they're the Raving Fan Builders.

Do It Yourself

If you click here, you can download the fulfillment continuum worksheet to brainstorm how to create leverage for client communication and relationships at scale.

When you look back at the fulfillment continuum concepts, the options for implementation are endless. We will cover some of those examples in greater detail in the Application chapter, but keep in mind that you want to review your offer cyclically to make sure you don't miss any opportunities for improvement.

Please use this worksheet so you can review this chapter yourself and apply the takeaways to your business and offers.

Click or go to the website: https://ethicalscaling.com/csm-book-downloads/

Scan me to download

Takeaways

When serving clients, you have one single goal, to keep them hooked. This term was popularized by Nir Eyal in his book *Hooked*.

Almost everyone spends the majority of their day on cruise control, based on habits that are hard-wired into their brains and that require little to no thought.

When you look at fulfillment and moving people across the continuum, you need to keep them hooked on a goal they aspire to enjoy.

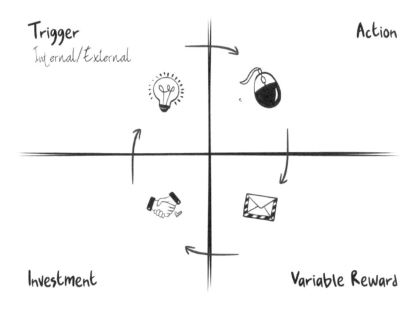

Being emotionally invested is the same as an escalation of commitment, which leads to Buy-in. That's what you want for a business that can scale to hundreds of active clients; you want it to be sticky.

Summary:

- Remember that knowing things are not how you want them to be can be a blessing, not a curse.

- When you feel like you're pushing the boulder up the mountain like Sisyphus, we give you permission to stop and reevaluate what you're doing.

- Clients won't care how much you know until they know how much you care.

- The Ideal Customer Engineer will be one of the most valuable assets for your business so you can both enroll great clients and also make all the others great.

- Ideal Customer Engineers help craft better client experiences to reach a broader audience instead of focusing on "perfect" clients.

- You should remember that in your client's journey, they're the hero, and you're just the guide.

- Fulfillment continuum analysis is the change that happens in the customer's mind going from being afraid and skeptical (buyer's remorse) to being engaged and committed (buy-in)

- Clients need to escalate their commitment to become biased towards action.

- Buy-in is the perfect synchronous moment between Emotion, Logic, and the Journey ahead.

- Expectation management is critical for keeping clients long-term.

How will you communicate this to your customers? Knowing

how to bucket them in different Archetypes and how to create Relationships at Scale with them will be key.

V. ARCHETYPES

The Foreign Jay

Let me reveal a simple fact about myself… I studied to become an Engineer, not only because I felt that it was the right thing for me but also because of how I'm wired. I'm a logical and systems thinker. It made total sense to go that route.

Everything for me will follow patterns, a path, and have some sequence that makes sense, even if it doesn't make sense for others. I am a builder and integrator at heart, and this has opened so many doors that I can't remember them all. But this also brought a lot of problems.

For most of my life, I assumed everyone was wired the same way until I learned that they weren't and that it was okay. I also figured out how big that handicap was because I was so invested in only half of my brain that I was missing a big piece: the emotional side, which has many essential skills.

I'd say that people that tend to be great at coaching other people are often the opposite of me. They don't love logic, numbers, or math, but they love people, the interactions, and learning how to serve others better.

It was time for me to learn how to work with people who were wired differently, and if that wasn't a skill that I was born with (like Ben), I'd own this skill in time.

I looked at archetypes and how people are wired the same way that I looked at learning another language. As a non-native English speaker born in Portugal and taught in school in another language that was not English, I was able to learn it. And I'm here today writing a book you can enjoy even if English is not my first language.

The same thing happened with archetypes. I learned to communicate in a "foreign" language that was not my central archetype. And it worked. It also worked for our clients, and we figured out it was repeatable. Are you excited to find out what the archetypes entail?

The Brain (not me)

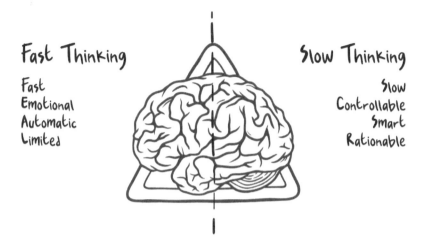

Fast Thinking

Fast
Emotional
Automatic
Limited

Slow Thinking

Slow
Controllable
Smart
Rationable

Let's go back to a concept back that I introduced in the Fulfillment Continuum: the Elephant and the Rider.

People don't have one or the other. They have a little bit of both. But everyone is wired differently, and they might have a dominant side. Let's call it a dominant brain hemisphere. And this will help you understand your customers, which ultimately creates that Relationship at Scale feeling you want.

In the last chapter, I covered in detail what the Buy-in process was, how we can help clients to be more committed, and how the three parts of that framework need to be in sync: logic, emotion, and the journey ahead.

Let's look at what lives on the two sides of the brains of our clients:

- The more logical side (slow thinking):

- o   Evidence-based.

- o   Rational.

- o   Looks for context.

- o   Searches for perspective.

- o   Judges based on shades of gray.

- o   Looks for self-fulfillment based on honesty, conscience, self-control, and purpose.

- The more emotional side (fast thinking):

- o   Based on opinions.

- o   Paranoid.

- o   Can become irrational.

- o   Emotive judgment.

- o   Black and White thinking.

- o   Looks for survival based on its instincts, drives, and vulnerability.

Understanding this makes fulfillment work so much easier because you can help your clients better understand what you're providing for them. And the more they care about something, the more they see it.

Of course, no one is only logical or emotional. You have them both and so do your clients. But you need to understand which qualities under logic or emotion are more prevalent and you can get clear on this by understanding the archetype of each individual client.

So your first step is to bucket clients, identifying which ones are more Analytical and Frontal Cortex based and which are more Emotional and Limbic System based.

Want to see the four archetypes?

The Four Archetypes

We will be referring to the following four archetypes:

- Doers and Controllers

    - The more rational minds tend to be super analytical and action-focused. Do well with numbers and love clarity.

    - Typically results-oriented, strong-willed, precise, and systematic.

- Worriers and Followers

    - The more emotional minds tend to go with feelings more and require some self-confidence build-up to create momentum.

- These archetypes love reassurance and support while craving human connection.

- Most of them are outgoing, enthusiastic, and tactful.

It's interesting as most people, after understanding these concepts, think Doers and Controllers are fast action-takers, but they usually use a slow thinking process. I mean that they're more deliberate with their actions and decisions, which makes them more rational.

This introduction to the archetypes will lay the groundwork for the most significant transformation you'll have in your business at scale. The archetypes allow you to create higher LTV, increase your retention and contract extensions, avoid drop-offs, and effectively delegate customer success to your fulfillment team.

Let's look a bit closer at the Archetypes.

Controllers and Doers have tons of self-confidence, are super-rational with their thinking, and tend to have a lot of energy and great performance. Although they have those traits, it's important for them to trust the process and you as a guide, which you'll find it's easier for Doers and harder for Controllers, Worriers and Followers.

Worriers and Followers tend to trust the process if you help them take action, and they feel seen and heard, but you'll deal with a lot of second-guessing of themselves.

So if Worriers and Followers are more emotional and connect more with that kind of communication, it's important not to fight them with logic and facts, which can make them indifferent to what you're saying. Otherwise, it will feel like you're sending a life vest to someone going through a tornado. The solution doesn't match the problem.

So all four archetypes have their traits. Each of them will bring their own challenges, and you'll be equipped with how to handle that effectively using what I am teaching you here.

Caveat: archetypes are not set in stone; they might change over time and vary across different phases and life events.

People can go from one to another and it should be seen as an ever-evolving framework because people are never static.

For example, a Follower can start showing up like a Doer or the opposite. Take a look at the overlapping in the graphic below:

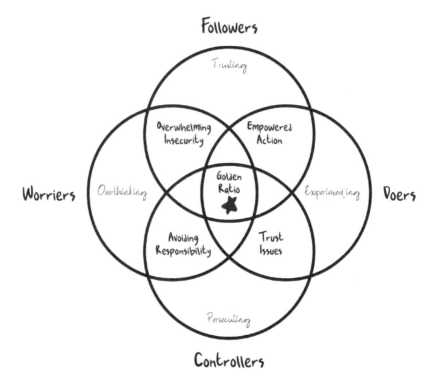

If you look at the extremes, you can see how different they can be. For example, Controllers can be obsessive in trying to create the new world they imagined. This unhealthy search for recognition and importance can put them in a state of burnout, and they end up blaming others for their circumstances.

A Follower can be the other extreme and can become a slave to acceptance. The overwhelming craving for social acceptance combined with their feeling of incapacity and hopelessness can sometimes make them feel like puppets. This keeps them from dreaming big.

In another instance, someone can be considered a Worrier if they spend too much time thinking and not much time doing. Worriers have an innate need to search for harsh truths that give them the certainty they crave. Uncertainty keeps them in their head as it means danger, and danger puts them out of any feeling of safety.

If Worriers go into more of a Controller mode, they are not only thinking a lot, they will start trying to rationalize it and second-guess all that you tell them. They will avoid any responsibility.

The same is true for a Follower who starts changing and showing up like a Doer, as they tend to trust and follow others. This archetype will feel more empowered to act and experiment.

Experiences from the past shape our clients' worldviews, so they tend to pay attention to things they're familiar with based on those past experiences. This is one of the reasons why Doers tend to be solution focused while Worriers tend to be more problem focused.

The golden ratio will be a combination of someone who believes in themselves, trusts you, and is willing to experiment. That's your Ideal Customer, and they can be self-maid.

Your Clients could be Self-maid Millionaires

Yes, you read it correctly, your clients can be self-maid millionaires. And no, this is not another grammar mistake I made because I'm a non-native English speaker! It's a story I want to share so you understand how people can change across different archetypes.

In 2007, a group of researchers decided to do something super interesting. They went to a hotel and analyzed what the maids were doing.

On average, the hotel maids were cleaning 15 rooms daily, averaging 20-30 minutes of cleaning per room. Quite challenging compared to me sitting and writing this book.

When the researchers asked whether any maids exercised, none had the time to do so, and none recognized their work as a form of exercise.

Now was the time for the researchers to test something. They told half of the maids about the benefits of exercising and that what they did as work could be considered a form of exercise.

They shared the same information on exercise benefits with the other half of the maids but did not reference their work as a form of exercise.

Now the exciting part: the researchers came back 4 weeks later to check with them to find that the first group who knew their work could be considered a form of exercise lost an average of 1.8 pounds. But group two lost none.

The big question arises: what was slimming these maids down?

It was one of the most potent drugs on earth, a placebo. Placebo is the perfect example of a self-maid drug.

This placebo gave the maids a more straightforward change process because they were already exercising, so if they did it a bit more vigorously (more conviction!), they could get even better results.

So yes, your clients could be like the maids and transform themselves when they believe change is more manageable than they thought. That's your role, to enable that transformation and get your clients in action, while keeping them confident and humble.

Confident Humility

What you want at the end of the day is what Adam Grant calls, in his book *Think Again, Confident Humility.*

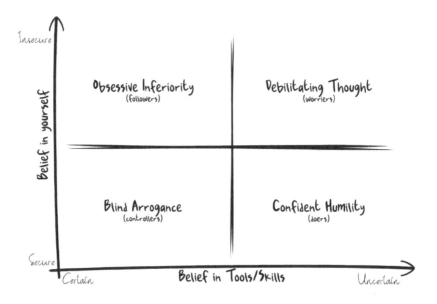

You want your client archetypes to have enough uncertainty around their knowledge and to know there is a margin to get better while being secure enough in themselves to be able to learn what's missing.

This graph can be transformative if you get it right, as it describes the focus of our work with clients.

A Controller might be too certain about what they know and lack awareness about what they don't know, leading them to arrogance. This explains why some of the clients you have are dropping off, and also why others are not extending their

178

contracts with you.

On the other hand, a Follower can be certain about what they know, but they're so insecure about themselves that they fall prey to obsessive inferiority.

Think about a Worrier for a second. They're insecure about themselves and uncertain about the skills and tools they need that they end up in a spiral of debilitating thoughts.

You will find, with Doers, that a healthy dose of uncertainty and self-confidence goes a long way, focusing more on getting better than being good. They'll be confident and humble.

But because things change over time, people can lose humility with experience, and that can transform many Doers into Controllers. I've fallen fell prey to that myself.

Jay under the microscope

Now that you can picture this in action, I will use myself as an example. For the most part, people know me for being a high performer, I get things done fast, and I am hyper-focused most of the time when working or doing something I love.

Most people I know would qualify me as a Doer, which isn't wrong. But I know myself better, and I'm not always a Doer.

I remember committing to my first high-ticket purchase, and I was freaking out. I was paying ten thousand dollars to be coached, and I was scared like a deer in headlights

But as soon as I understood the process I was going through, I switched to being a Doer. The story doesn't end there... I was entering a field I didn't completely understand and had a lack of confidence that brought the Worrier inside of me to the forefront.

That's not the only time it happened; I have plenty of examples of me being on other sales calls where I wasn't a Worrier. I became a Controller. I knew how the field worked. I understood the game's rules so that I could start bending reality.

In some of those sales calls, after my first High Ticket purchase, being a Controller was not meant to be annoying but to be in Control. I wanted to understand what the offer was and how that was connected to the Big Outcome I had in mind while also making sure I could trust the process and believe that goal was attainable. After testing the sales person, I would switch back to Doer if I felt confident in what they were saying.

See how exciting archetypes can be? This is one-size-fits-all! Okay, maybe not.

Mindset and Strategies that apply to all Archetypes

One-size-fits-all is usually the wrong approach, but I want to drop some nuggets that work for any humans you deal with. We will, of course, spend time reviewing the particulars of each archetype in the following chapters.

One of the most common pieces of feedback I've heard in this space is that when clients don't get results, it's their mindset. I usually laugh and think about how minimalistic this approach is. It's so vague and lacks ownership from the business offering the service.

But it's not totally false either. Clients need to be challenged for them to grow and tackle bigger challenges in the future, but it's hard to get everyone to buy into this growth mindset.

You can help them go through a transformation. When you're present, you remind clients that they will struggle, that they will fail, and that they might feel defeated, but that throughout that journey, they will get better and succeed in the end.

I remember this from a personal experience. When I was in my sophomore year, I was already an engineer without knowing it. My Math grades were always excellent because it felt like second nature to me.

But during that sophomore year, I was challenged to enter a new

Math program, which I immediately did without knowing what was in store for me. This unique program was much more difficult than anything I had ever tried before!

Sophomore and junior year were tough to adapt to because the difficulty level was out of this world, which almost made me second-guess my math skills. The funny part was when I got to senior year and had to prepare for exams, things started getting easier.

During the National exam, I got one of the best grades in the country, all due to being able to endure a demanding challenge that ended up making me stronger.

So a significant portion of why clients get results or not is related to their mindset, and one of the big things I've seen working against a great offer is a client's mindset, specifically when they get pessimistic. This is what most business owners mean when they say that their client's problem is their mindset.

Maybe the way you perceive pessimism might be different from mine, so I'll break down the three aspects of it:

- **Personalization**: seeing everything that happens as their fault.

    - *"This is my fault, and this is awful."*

    - Clients start to believe that they're at fault for whatever has gone wrong in the process, and they end up confusing lack of preparation with incompetence.

- The perfect reframe would be to help them think: *"it may look difficult, but first, we try it and see."*

- **Generalization**: making one small thing bigger than it needs to be.

  - *"My whole life is awful."*

  - Clients expect a small problem to affect all areas of their life due to human biases.

  - The perfect reframe would be to help them think: *"This may look hard, but have you ever thought about all the things you've mastered?"*

- **Perpetuation:** this happens when they think a verb becomes an identity.

  - *"And it's gonna always be awful."*

  - Clients think that the problem they're facing will stay forever, and they perpetuate it with their subjective bias; they see their failing (a verb) as them becoming a failure (identity).

  - The perfect reframe would be to help them think: *"some things feel hard, but with practice, they get easier."*

Equipped with this knowledge, you can pay attention to changes in your client's language patterns to understand if they're entering a very dangerous mindset or frame of mind. This will be reflected in their behaviors and communication styles, and I want you to be aware of that. Your goal as their leader is to find what is working and how you can replicate success instead of trying to win an argument that doesn't serve you or the client.

You then can help clients embody the success behaviors that will propel them forward, like motivation, perseverance, time management, work habits, and willingness to ask for feedback and support. You're not teaching intelligence. That is entirely out of your control, but you're teaching them self-discipline, self-regulation, and grit.

So what mindsets do your clients need?

Here are the four mindsets you want to install in your client's minds:

- **Belonging:** This is a big part of what we covered as one of the key drivers and meanings behind the big outcome.

    ○ *"I belong in this community."*

    ○ Make them feel they are part of something bigger than themselves, make them feel seen and heard, and get them to engage in group activities while fostering peer-to-peer interactions.

- **Ability**: This helps reduce the perception of effort over time.

  - *"My ability and competence grow with my effort."*

  - This is also known as a growth mindset, and we can foster that when we find opportunities to teach them how to focus on being better instead of being good.

- **Self-efficacy:** This is a key piece that falls under the belief umbrella, which is pivotal to more emotional archetypes like Worriers or Followers.

  - *"I can succeed at this."*

  - Competence breeds confidence, so as Ideal Customer Engineers, we want to act as a feedback loop and reinforce the idea they can do it.

- **Expectancy:** This is a mix of connecting effort with the goal, and expectation management, while also playing with the belief they need to take action.

  - *"This work is valuable."*

  - Understanding your clients, and getting to their root motivators, will allow them to see the value behind all of their efforts. This is why a Big Outcome without meaning will make expectancy hard to plant as a mindset.

Any archetype will benefit from you teaching them successful behaviors for the big outcome they want but also for life. Let's start the first Archetype Clinic and see some of these concepts in action.

Archetype Clinic

From a client of ours:

"Our client success director has fully embraced this, and it has been a huge asset to our company! Things are so much easier, not only from a delivery point but also, we've become less judgmental about our clients and ourselves".

This consulting client was doing great with acquisition when we started working together, but their offer worked for some of their clients and didn't for others. A subgroup of clients kept struggling with taking action, which made it hard for them to perceive any value from the offer. In turn, they were struggling to keep clients.

A simple process like introducing archetypes and labeling them from the beginning helped them cater their communication style, implementation pathways, and action plans to create a next-level experience for their clients..

You're probably already seeing how this works and how you

could apply it immediately. At the surface level, that will give you some immediate results and a sense of control, but we want to go deeper. Let's keep peeling back the layers of the onion to find out the frames of mind and how they'll apply to each archetype.

Drama Triangle

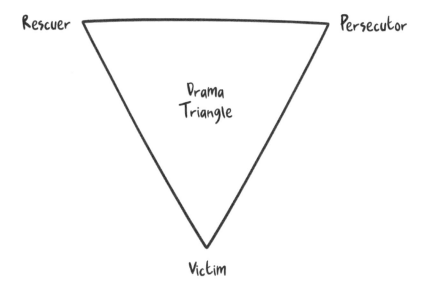

This chapter is getting heavier in concepts, but please bear with me. It will all come together in the next chapter, where we will analyze how to apply this to each individual archetype.

The Drama Triangle, also known as Karpman's Triangle, is very popular in the coaching space. It's pretty self-explanatory; for every interaction, people will play one of three roles: Persecutor,

Victim, or Rescuer.

Imagine it like this: the Drama Triangle and its roles are like a hat that any archetype can wear. It doesn't change the person but changes how they show up and how you perceive them.

Basically, for every Persecutor, there will be a Victim, and for every Victim, there will be a Rescuer.

As Ideal Customer Engineers, you can embody a little bit of each when interacting with clients, so you'll know how to keep yourself in a position of power and leadership.

Persecutor

It's interesting to understand how the Drama Triangle can change Relationships at Scale and how it will make you a better human being, even when managing relationships with your family and friends.

We have all dealt with someone acting like a Persecutor, typically with one or several of the following characteristics:

- Overcritical.

- Blaming everyone.

- Rigid thinking.

- Me-first approach.

- They'll use expressions like:

  - *It's your fault.*

  - *What are you thinking?*

  - *Why did you do that?*

  - *What's your problem?*

This is also known, in some circles, as the Alpha Wolf mindset, where someone thinks they own the world, that others are usable, has almost zero tolerance for people, and thinks that compassion is a weakness. They tend to lead with aggression and hostility.

When someone shows up like this, you shouldn't play that game. As for every Persecutor, there is a Victim and you don't want to be the Victim. Controllers use this role as a Persecutor to help them hold a strong frame in interactions with you, as they usually test you and validate your trustworthiness.

Worriers can show up as if they're so desperate that the only way out is to blame you for their lack of results. Let's take a closer look at what the Victim hat looks like.

Victim

I have a small group of friends today and within that group I can easily see the ones who love a Victim because Victims are often the perfect person for a Coach. Coaches can love being a Rescuer. It makes them feel helpful and valuable. Victims typically have one or several of the following characteristics:

- Helpless.

- Ashamed.

- Can't solve problems.

- Avoid responsibility.

- They'll use expressions like:

  - *Poor me!*

  - *I'm not responsible.*

  - *I don't know what to do.*

  - *They don't like me.*

  - *Why is this happening to me?*

This is also known in some circles as the Snow White mindset, where someone shows up like a passive victim who has no responsibility or power to change things.

This is the typical approach Worriers use. If they're a Victim and show up helpless, they feel they should have no responsibility for the outcomes. They usually try to get you to do for them what they don't want to do, and it's easy to fall for that trap.

Some Followers can also use this frame, depending on how helpless they're feeling in other areas of their life, so you need to keep an eye on it. You'll understand this in more depth in the coming chapters.

Rescuer

Most fulfillment team members confuse what coaching is and what being a Rescuer means. Those roles are different, and as Ideal Customer Engineers, you want to coach and empower people, not save them. They're the hero, remember?

Rescuers tend to follow some of the following patterns:

- Over-helpful.

- Sacrifice for others.

- Create Codependency.

- Feels capable when rescuing.

- Attach self-worth to the feedback gotten from the other person.

- They'll use expressions like:

    o *Let me help you.*

    o *I will do that.*

- ○ *Let's not fight…*

- ○ *I feel bad for you.*

- ○ *You will be fine.*

This is the typical frame used by Followers, they want to look nice, and because they're more emotional than logical, they love and crave human connection. It's also the excuse they use not to introspect and get their stuff together. This will be the typical smokescreen when you feel like a Follower is stuck.

Other examples are when your customer success team tries to over-deliver and make up for any flaws in the offer they're aware of. They tend to over-coach and rescue, and that's not healthy for them or the business.

Enough Drama

Now that you have a baseline for what the Drama Triangle means, I will show you how to "Flip the Script" for every archetype in the following chapters.

For you to flip the script, you will be going from The Drama Triangle to The Empowered Dynamic.

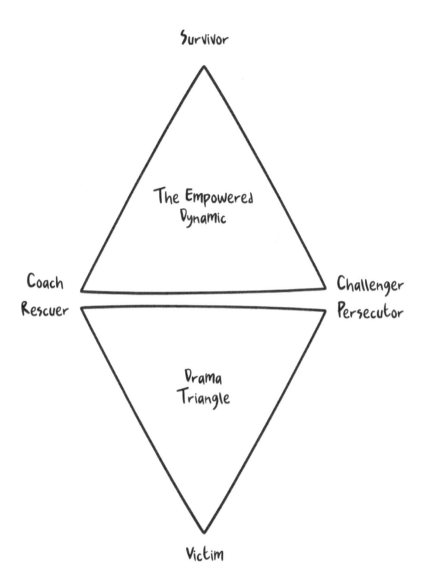

This will help the Ideal Customer Engineer, you, your team or both, to keep the focus on being a guide, not a hero. Because now and then, you might feel the urge to be a rescuer, you must remember that the goal is to be a guide for clients.

As their Ideal Customer Engineer, you won't focus on rescuing them but on coaching them through your process. You can do that by providing reassurance, making sure you don't do for them what they can do for themselves, having clear boundaries and limitations, and ensuring you only help when asked to do so.

But you will have that urge. The desire for rescuing arises when there is Victim energy present. That Victim can become a Survivor and hero with the right tools, and we will cover that soon.

Flipping the Script for an Archetype

In the following chapters, you will apply these concepts individually to all the archetypes and frames of mind from the Drama Triangle.

This will enable your fulfillment team to have the detail and knowledge to explore these tough conversations and opportunities. These scenarios will have tension and can feel like inflection points in the client journey, but when done well, they will plant a seed in your customer's mind: they will have a better path forward in working with you.

Helping your clients understand reality from their perception under stress is an act of leadership, and as Chip and Dan Heath call it, it's an opportunity for clients to trip over the truth. Helping your clients shape a new worldview will shape their behaviors that, at the end of the day, will inform their results. I don't love the idea of just telling clients what they need to hear, I prefer to show them what they need to see. Helping them experience realizations and epiphanies creates stronger memories and establish a new identity even faster. This helps your clients appreciate your solutions because they learn how to enjoy the problem beforehand.

So for you as an owner, your team that works with clients, and for clients, these moments will be vital.

These moments place you in situations where you can fail, and that's okay. Your goal is to be better, make your team better, and your clients great.

Now it's your turn.

Do It Yourself

Download the archetype summary and start brainstorming, by yourself or with your team, on how you can start the application of these concepts, how to create implementation pathways and action plans, and adjust your communication style.

Please use this worksheet so you can review this chapter yourself and apply your takeaways to your business and offers.

Click or go to the website: https://ethicalscaling.com/csm-book-downloads/

Scan me to download

Start by going through your client roster:

- Explain to everyone involved in the delivery process what the four archetypes are.

- Get the fulfillment team to go through all of your active clients and label them with one of the four archetypes.

- For each client, and archetype, document how successful that client has been so far while working with you.

- Check for trends to see if some of the archetypes tend to do better than others.

- Brainstorm different ways to serve clients that will allow them to define their pace and deliver results faster and more aligned with how they're wired.

This exercise should be fairly simple and will make the next section much easier.

Takeaways

It has been a long journey so far. I know the concepts I've shared could be new and different from what you have seen before. It will all make sense after going through all the Clinics in this book and implementing them.

Summary:

- Our brain has two main sides: Fast and Slow, Rational and Emotional.

- Fast is emotional and more automatic.

- Slow is the rationale, and smarter.

- We bucket clients into 4 main archetypes: Doers and Controllers, Worriers and Followers.

- Doers are more logical and have high self-confidence, but they also understand they don't have all the skills or answers.

- Controllers are also logical and self-confident, but they tend to think they know more than they do.

- Worriers are more emotional and usually don't trust themselves or their skills, leading to paralysis.

- Followers are also more emotional and trust their skills but, generally speaking, not themselves enough, leading to unhealthy levels of inferiority.

- All archetypes can play any role in the Drama Triangle, so it's essential to address them as Frames of Mind they use under stress, like wearing a hat for different occasions.

Va. DOER

Gradual and Consistent Improvement

"Success isn't always about greatness. It's about consistency.
Consistent hard work leads to success. Greatness will come."

Dwayne Johnson

Saturday Night Fever

It was 2014, actually, to be specific, the 14th of June, a Saturday.

I was sitting at home chilling, scrolling through my Facebook feed, when a notification popped. "You have a new message," it said.

I clicked, and it was weird. It was a new message for my brand-new Facebook Business page. It was a few days old, and I had been spinning my wheels around this new health project, slowly and steadily trying to understand how to create a page and blog.

It had 0 followers, and I wanted it that way until I felt confident it could be shared with the world. But someone found it... "Is this some of Zuck's trickery, I thought?"

After going through this inner chatter, I decided to open the DM. It said: "what services do you offer?"

Services? I don't even know how to run this page properly yet, but I was excited, puzzled, and overwhelmed all at once. The page hadn't even launched, and I got my first lead, looking for help, and it looked like my dream avatar.

A 35ish woman with a mom-like appearance was looking for support on how to lose weight and reshape her body again. Seemed too good to be true, but it was happening.

After thinking about it for a couple of hours, I decided to throw spaghetti at the wall and see what would stick.

I explained that we were launching a project and that we had been working with a handful of people, and described what kind of work and results could be expected. She agreed that that was exactly what she wanted and asked for prices.

I dropped the price, details for payment, and we agreed on starting next week. It was a breeze.

I'll remember this client forever because this client is exactly what I think of when talking about a Doer.

If you go back to the *Your Book Guide section*, I described the diffusion of innovation. Doers, commonly but not always, tend to fit either in the Innovators or Early Adopters category. This archetype tends to love novelty, and they value being the first over the certainty of a proven system.

Doers are what makes your offer take off quickly, as not only do they like new ideas, but take lots of action. They're also guilty of making you believe the initial offer and approach will work for everyone.

Whenever you catch yourself thinking. "For those who do the work, my process works."

What you're saying is: For Doers, my process works.

But unless you want to keep serving a tiny market niche, what helped you take off won't work for the future. This is why we have four archetypes.

Let's understand how to best communicate and serve a Doer before we figure out the remaining archetypes.

Serving a Doer

Working with a Doer is like being a football coach and having the best player you could ask for: someone with outstanding performance and an incredible work ethic.

But those are the top 1%, or maybe even less than 1%. They're hard to find, and there aren't enough to sustain your business long-term. Although they have all these great traits, there are still a few things to keep in mind to make sure they spread the word and attract more eyeballs on what you do, and as Doers, they'll be more than happy to record a testimonial that can attract other clients.

When searching for help and support, a Doer is looking for clarity. They want someone with the assertiveness to communicate what needs to be done with a clear and detailed action plan.

While dealing with Doers, we know that they will have no trouble dealing with phases of stress and uncertainty because they will push through, which can give you an edge when you catch them wanting to go faster.

On top of that, Doers tend to not be risk averse, so asking them to do challenging tasks, even risky ones, can put them in the right frame of mind. And they're quick to take action. That's a nice bonus.

The beginning of the journey with a Doer can be transformative when you understand what is most important to them and ensure they are on track with the actions they are taking, giving them a clear focus.

This archetype is probably the easiest of them all, but we still want them to feel seen and heard like any other client. Just because they don't ask for much help, you can't forget that a continuous feedback loop is necessary to guarantee they are clear about their action steps and they feel cared for.

Help them stay the course while not inhibiting their momentum.

Flipping the Script for a Doer

Remember, Doers fall under the umbrella of logical thinkers, and a Doer can show up like a Controller when things don't go well, he doesn't feel taken care of, or he lacks clarity.

Here is a simple guide to serving this archetype well:

- Be detailed with your answers and feedback.

- Provide recognition.

- Answer the how.

- Use data and stats whenever possible.

- Provide Logic and Facts.

- Stress reliability on both ends of this interaction.

If you have a client that's a Doer, but you feel like their level of trust is lower, and they might be second guessing everything, there is a chance they're switching to Controller, so please refer to the section on Flipping the Script for a Controller.

Serving a Doer Clinic

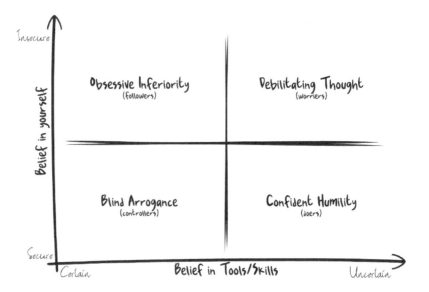

I remember this situation like it was yesterday. I had the great opportunity to work with one of the fastest-growing companies in the high-ticket service industry.

They hired us to help with fulfillment. The owner is a marketing and sales-focused person who has been able to almost 10x every year since he started.

I was lucky to work with the Client Success Director, his brother. It was a great experience; I saw he was a Doer from day one.

I can say that he was the one who challenged me to focus on calling this archetype a Doer since we've revamped the names over time.

The work with him was easy because we focused on what mattered to him, allowing him to experiment with a few tactics, understand if the strategy was going in the right direction, and finally support him in the implementation process.

Remember what Doers want: *enough trust in you to keep experimenting with the tools and skills you're sharing with them without dealing with setbacks.*

I know I won't only work with clients like this, and that's okay. We can have great moments with other archetypes too.

Do It Yourself

This exercise is a continuation of the one you started in the introduction of the archetypes chapter. You can go deeper now that you know more about how Doers are wired.

Please use this worksheet so you can review this chapter yourself and be clear on your big takeaways to apply them to your business and offers.

Click or go to the website: https://ethicalscaling.com/csm-book-downloads/

Scan me to download

Start by going through your client roster:

- Now that you have a client roster labeled with archetypes, identify the Doers.

- Check if the majority of them got great results while working with you.

- Also, check how many of them were renewed or upgraded to a different offer.

- Equipped with the knowledge you have now, what would you do differently in the future when working with a Doer?

You know this can be the easiest archetype to work with, but let's not ignore them. Keeping them on track is still important.

Takeaways

Doers tend to understand how life works and how they must

show up. If you help them slowly and gradually go from one level to the next, they will be happy.

Doers tend to deal well with being on a plateau if they understand why, and they'll keep practicing even when no progress is visible.

Summary:

- Doers tend to have outstanding performance and work ethic.

- There are not enough Doers in the marketplace to sustain a business that wants to cross the chasm and scale.

- Doers benefit from Clarity and Direction.

- They're usually logical thinkers, but when uncertain about you, can become Controllers.

Sadly, the world isn't made up solely of Doers, and I'll risk saying they're the 1% of the population or even less, so if you want to expand your reach, impact, and profits, you need to understand how to guide the other three archetypes too.

Vb. CONTROLLER

Obsessively from bump to bump

"Our thoughts shape us. We become our obsessions. Our thoughts can enslave us or save us."

Kilroy J. Oldster

Freakajay

It was 7 am in the morning, staring at the horizon… Opening my fancy Leuchtturm 1917 journal, recognized as the "better classic Moleskine" notebook with horizontal and vertical lines.

A couple of boxes, dots, circles, and squares. My bullet journal was looking great.

I went over my week and thought about my goals, which tasks were a priority, and which were my non-negotiables. This made me feel great! This was in 2017, and I still use a similar process today.

This has been a keystone habit in my high-performance routine. It might feel rigid for some, but that rigidity gave me the process and constraints that would help me get all my work done consistently and live the work week I always wanted: working five hours a day, four days a week while building a business that I loved.

I remember sharing this process with my girlfriend, waiting for her to say how great I was, only to find her saying: "you're a total control freak." She wasn't wrong. I was and I can still be at times today.

Those moments bring the Controller in me to the surface, the one that likes rigidity, specificity, and granularity and sometimes can make me miss the forest for the trees. I'm happy I'm surrounded by people that can help me keep my reality in check.

Serving a Controller like I am can sometimes be a challenge. But how can you spot a Controller apart from their Moleskine notebook?

Serving a Controller

Controllers are one of a kind, and although my experience says most customer success people hate this archetype, I love working with them. You might be asking yourself, why?

Archetypes are not static, people change. And a Controller is the closest to becoming a Doer. So, when you understand that, you know you have an opportunity to get more people to get the results they want with your process. Controllers can become the ones that take massive action and become great success stories.

Of course, there is some work to do to make that happen. Controllers tend to look promising early on. Their thirst for success makes them highly focused and attentive to whatever happens.

This kind of person doesn't accept being the second-best. They're hyper focused on results; it doesn't matter how they achieve them. They want it to be fast and to happen now.

The Controller wants, whenever possible, to learn everything in the first lesson, so they don't need to wait to get the returns.

As soon as they start a new challenge, as soon as they understand there is some effort that needs to be invested, they'll find their first results, but at the same time, they will find their first plateau. Remember that after every peak, there will be a valley.

This is the first time they need to double down on effort, but their lack of understanding of limits makes them forget the word "moderation." Instead, they'll take shortcuts or put in extra hours to get those results. I'm guilty of being a Controller for most of my life, so I know how it feels.

When things go great, Controllers usually don't stop and celebrate. They ignore it. But when something goes wrong, they spend energy like a madman thinking about it. When I had moments of being overly focused on problems, an external perspective that brought attention to solutions helped me zoom out and avoid spinning my wheels.

This level of unsustainable effort creates some results and progress, followed by moments of setbacks (due to the unsustainability). Energy starts to wane, and controllers fall into the abyss. And then they quit; they stop trusting the process.

This obsessiveness some Controllers have creates a risk of them injuring themselves, mainly on an emotional level. Just think about it, how many times have you met a client like this? Or a friend? That would hustle and grind at all costs?

This urge to control, to have continued success, is dangerous. How can you work with this archetype to move them from obsession and stubbornness to openness and being coachable?

Well, first of all, you need to pay attention to their patterns. If this archetype starts asking questions, a lot of them, it means they are not crystal clear on the outcomes they can get in the future if they stick to the process. Remember, Controllers have no problem trusting themselves. They might have a hard time trusting you or the process.

Also, because Controllers tend to have a big ego and high levels of self-confidence, if by any means they sense your team lacks confidence, they'll crush them. And not only that, they'll try to change the process to fit their beliefs and worldviews while making you or your team commit to their plans instead of sticking to the process. Controllers will bend your reality.

Controllers usually have trust issues, so we need to ensure that trust is being built, thus why we refer to Relationships at Scale so often. This archetype also benefits from the relationship-building process.

The easiest way to start helping this archetype shift to a more manageable one is to make sure you set clear expectations early on and meet them where they are at every step of the journey; this will help them trust you more while becoming more coachable.

One of the best ways to help them stay out or get out of obsessions, hustling, and grinding is to help them zoom out and move away from granular thinking. Imagine they're a horse using blinders, and you're the one removing those blinders.

Those minor tweaks, and understanding of the archetype, connected to the frameworks in the fulfillment continuum, will help win this client over. They will want to stay with you for life because they tend to back off controlling over time when they trust and become a Doer.

Flipping the Script for a Controller

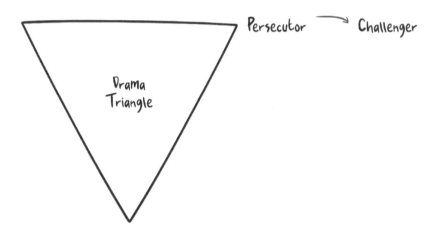

Persecutor — Challenger

Drama Triangle

You must remember that the Controller is super analytical and has a strong Rider that I referred to in the Buy-in process. Usually, what gets them stuck and misbehaving is that they're in analysis paralysis. The plethora of options available will cause willpower depletion.

Although controllers are sharp and have had some past successes, when they experience doubt or exhaustion, they'll do what everyone does: go back to default, following the path of least resistance. And this lack of clarity creates a lot of resistance which generates conflict.

Controllers, when conflict starts, tend to go in the direction of being a Persecutor. Your goal is to reframe them from Persecutor to Challenger, making your communication more efficient and helping the client to regain momentum.

You have a few things to remember when this archetype shows up like that.

For Controllers showing up like a Persecutor, your communication needs to be assertive with no vague ideas or questions. It's essential to be direct and concise for them to understand your point of view and to be open to the challenge at hand.

Also, because Controllers will try to control whenever they can, you need to set clear boundaries on what you can do for them and what you can't. There is nothing wrong with communicating boundaries with this archetype in order to communicate clearly from the beginning. We should manage their expectations appropriately.

A simple way for you to interact with a Controller when they're wearing their Persecutor hat is just to allow them to share what they have to say. Give them space to vent. As their Ideal Customer Engineer, you should let them go without interruption and use active listening to understand what they're really saying.

After they talk out loud and feel like you're not buying into the conflict, it will enable you to ask some great questions. Questions that go to the root cause will allow them to open up, and you can explore solutions within your boundaries.

We love using questions from The Coaching Habit by Michael Bungay Stanier, as it helps us navigate these tough conversations with our own clients.

An example would be to ask them, "what's the real challenge here?" after they go on a tangent about everything that is turning them off. And you can ask another question around boundaries, saying something like, "I can't do that, but I could do this instead. Can we brainstorm an action plan together?".

But beware, questions are tricky for Controllers. If you overuse them and they feel like this is an interrogation, this will generate more anger, the urge to persecute, and a feeling of a lack of progress.

So whenever you feel like questions aren't working, you can flip the script and use mirroring. Just state what you're saying and ask them to confirm that you understood them correctly.

Feel free to use some of their words and a deeper breakdown of what you hear, and let them confirm that that is what they mean or not. Never assume you know the truth. They're the only ones who know what's on their minds.

Here is a simple guide to serving this archetype well:

- Be direct and straightforward.

- Keep your boundaries clear.

- Be brief and to the point.

- Answer the <u>what</u> (don't stress the how).

- The goal is the result (trust).

- Focus on logic.

- Agree with the facts they share, not necessarily with them.

Keep in mind that although this is typical for Controllers, they might also show up like Victims depending on what has happened in their life. If you feel your Controller client is showing up like a Victim, please refer to the Flipping the Script for a Worrier section.

Serving a Controller Clinic

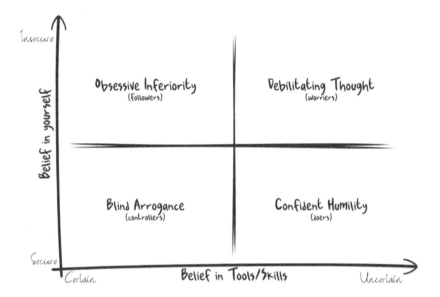

As I said before, controllers can be a challenge I embrace and love. I like to keep in mind that I cannot attach my self-worth to any outcomes with a Controller or any client for that matter.

You now know how easy it is for them to be arrogant even without that intention. It's a symptom that shows their lack of trust in your tools and skills.

I remember we had a client not long ago that was a Controller. Although in some early interactions, he showed up a bit overwhelmed, I could feel whenever there was space, he'd try to bend our reality.

He'd try to change our process a bit to fit within his worldview. That's the Controller vibe. But knowing what we know about this archetype, we knew the goal was to give him some quick wins that would help this client trust us enough to implement the action plan consistently.

If we confused him with a Worrier that lacks belief in himself, we would have been reassuring someone that didn't need much reassurance instead of focusing on what mattered to him.

Do It Yourself

This exercise is a continuation of the one you started in the introduction of the archetypes chapter. You can go deeper now that you know more about how Controllers are wired.

Please use this worksheet so you can review this chapter yourself and use your takeaways to apply this to your business and offers.

Click or go to the website: https://ethicalscaling.com/csm-book-downloads/

Scan me to download

Start by going through your client roster:

- Now that you have a client roster labeled with archetypes, identify the Controllers.

- Check if the majority of them got great results while working with you.

- Also, check how many of them were renewed or upgraded to a different offer.

- Check if you got drop-outs or refunds from any Controllers.

- Equipped with the knowledge you have now, what would you do differently in the future when working with a Controller?

Controllers are the closest to Doers; keep that in mind. You have a chance to convert them and make them Raving Fans.

Takeaways

After auditing and working as a Consultant for over a hundred different businesses, I can say the consensus is that most coaches and account managers dislike working with Controllers. It's likely because they feel threatened.

Controllers are very logical, as I said before, so when you think about the Buy-in Framework, their rational brain (rider) tends to be the strongest. And that's not necessarily a bad thing! We must remember who the rider is and that he has many strengths: a great thinker, a prolific planner, and a hard worker to make the vision become a reality.

The biggest challenge is their tendency to spin their wheels and overanalyze. This creates a significant problem: hyperfocus on difficulties.

The Controller will benefit from your support in providing direction: telling them where to go, how to act, and explaining the path to the destination. You will increase trust whenever you explore their past success to help them replicate what they've done that worked well in this new journey with you.

That extra clarity provided to Controllers can get them in the right headspace. For some Controllers, even success can feel like a pitfall, and those pitfalls make them feel like losers. So don't let their energy mess up your confidence; like any other archetype, a solution for a Controller is rarely a Big Solution. That's not how you solve a Big Problem.

With a Controller, engineering a sequence of steps that can be built on will go a long way, focusing on what works and doing more. Don't focus on fixing them when the journey or the archetype is broken.

When empowered with the knowledge of how to deal with Controllers and with the hope that they can become Doers, your team won't be nervous or fearful about working with this archetype any longer.

Summary:

- Controllers are the closest to a Doer.

- They're usually sharp and promising early on in their journey with you.

- Can become obsessed with results.

- Have a massive urge to feel in control.

- Typically have trust issues.

- Benefits from zooming out.

- Assertive communication is key.

Vc. WORRIER

Starting over and over again

"Our thoughts make us what we are."

Dale Carnegie

Monks know it better

It was a long walk late in the day, and two monks were tired and thirsty. After a long day, they just wanted to return to the monastery.

There had been heavy rain and there was water everywhere. The river flowed like crazy, and the two monks needed to cross it before reaching the monastery.

When they were getting close to one side of the river, they found a woman staring at the water, unable to cross the river to the other side. Confused, the younger Monk asked her why she was staring at the water and not crossing the river to the other side, only to find out the young woman didn't know how to swim.

The elder of the two Monks picked her up and carried her on his back to the other side of the river, leaving her and then continuing his journey in silence to the monastery.

Tired of that long day, the silence, and puzzled about what happened, the young Monk couldn't stop himself and asked the elder Monk: "Sir, as monks, shouldn't we avoid touching a woman?"

The elder Monk promptly responded, "yes, we should."

Then the younger Monk asks again: "But then, Sir, how is it that you carried that woman from one side of the river to the other?"

The elder Monk smiled at him and said, "I left her on the other side of the river, but you're still carrying her."

Worriers can be everywhere, even in the heart of a young Monk.

Serving a Worrier

Worriers are a peculiar client archetype. This kind of person takes on any new challenge with lots of enthusiasm and loves novelty! They crave new engineered hope.

Although they love a new challenge, that excitement fades away fast. This leads them to quit what they just started, telling everyone around them that this thing they just started was not aligned with their "personal needs."

The Worrier loves to be a Star, and as soon as he quits, he still loves feeling special, so if something doesn't work out, it's never his fault. He'll find a new shiny object and restart the enthusiasm cycle again. The grass is always greener on the other side, right?

He finds the new grass and excitement till the new plateau hits, and he quits again. The cycle repeats itself.

The Worrier thinks of himself as an adventurer, but he's nothing more than an eternal child who cannot take full responsibility and ownership of his life.

How often have you felt someone in your close circle was in a loop like this?

How many clients have you dealt with that show up as Worriers?

Have you been guilty of being a Worrier yourself?

That's the most crucial part of the process; clients can all fall prey to becoming a Worrier. If you want to look for symptoms, the following are some things to keep in mind:

- Has a lot of questions.

- Wonders, "is this going to work for me?"

- Wants predictability and security.

- Has more risk aversion than other types of clients.

So you can feel they're a potential Worrier whenever a client asks a lot of questions, typically long ones and/or judgmental ones.

They're full of uncertainty, typically around themselves. And because they're so risk averse, they'll feel like the safe bet is to stay put. I touched on this when I discussed escalation of commitment and erroneous abandonment in the previous chapters, and the high risks and low perceived responsibility can lead them to quit and drop off.

Understanding that almost all of these clients are confused, tired, exhausted, and overwhelmed will help us change how we show up. They don't want to show up like a Worrier for fun, they're probably not even aware of it.

Although some days might be a challenge when serving a Worrier, you can be more preventative in working with them.

One of the first things you can do with a Worrier is to answer questions before they ask. When you know what specific inflection points will create uncertainty, you can normalize failure and explain what will work for them and how they'll feel.

Also, understand that for Worriers, communication is vital, as they get overwhelmed easily, and it's hard for them to connect the dots and see where things are going trajectory-wise. If you paint the connection between today and tomorrow, they feel more empowered to take action.

There will be moments of doubt, typically doubt about themselves. These moments for this archetype will create an opportunity for you to reassure them and help them avoid the pessimistic route. Remember that the service only has value if they believe it's doable and that the goals are attainable.

Flipping the Script for a Worrier

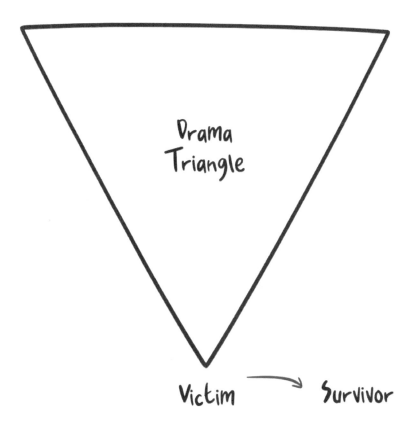

Worriers, when overwhelmed, tend to go into a Victim frame of mind. Our goal is to reframe them from Victim to Survivor, which will make our communication more efficient and helps the client to regain momentum.

Worriers benefit significantly from you reassuring them whenever things don't go as planned, as this helps them trust themselves more or at least not to lose the little self-confidence they have.

You should also remember that reassuring them is not the same as guiding them to do what they can do for themselves. Worriers must know your boundaries and limitations and know that you should only help when asked.

After understanding the archetypes, you'll have a good understanding and gut instinct on how and when to help a Worrier.

One thing that can help Worriers when giving them feedback is asking permission-based questions. Instead of going all in and being overly assertive with feedback, like you would for a Controller, you ask for permission first.

"Would you be okay with me giving you some feedback on this?"

When they give you permission, the feedback will be better received because they asked for it.

Another option to explore when things aren't going great for Worriers is to remember their self-confidence is fragile, so our advice can further harm their confidence. What is proven to work better for this archetype is to ask them to advise others.

If you can find something about the Worrier that they know and trust themselves about, help them share that, help them share their wisdom. This will make your Worrier feel more intelligent and capable of assisting others in feeling like a role model and a person who can succeed.

Here is a simple guide to serving this archetype well:

- Be friendly and relaxed.

- Allow them to do most of the talking and rapport-building early on.

- Translate ideas into actions (get them out of their head).

- Answer the who (build responsibility).

- Stress the new and special (tap into the novelty they love).

- Avoid being dominating.

- Quote experts and testimonials for better-perceived authority (conformity bias).

Worriers might also show up like Persecutors depending on what has happened in their life. If you feel your Worrier client is showing up like a Persecutor, please refer to the Flipping the Script for a Controller section.

Serving a Worrier Clinic

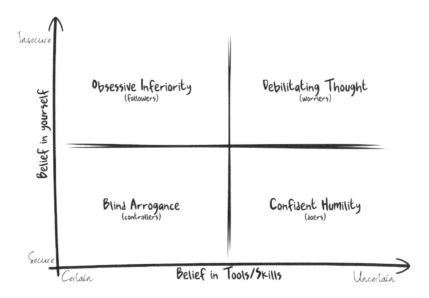

You know how debilitating thought can prevent this archetype from taking action, and empowered with that knowledge, that's one of the first things you should address.

We had a client a couple of years ago, probably one of the first ones joining this offer, who was a clear Worrier.

He showed up late for most calls and missed a few messages, and I could feel his bandwidth was taxed enough for him to struggle with any more work.

After a couple of interactions during our consulting work together, I could barely see any progress. After the calls, he still needed to do some implementation with his team, but I couldn't see anything being properly implemented. I started to feel he was going back to no commitment, which would destroy any goals we had in mind.

I took some time to reflect, and I came up with one idea on how we could at least get some stuff implemented that could change their business for the better. Next call we had booked, I probed him and tried to find out who the implementer on their team was and if he would be okay with me meeting with him and discussing how I could help this person implement some of our actions.

He liked the idea and connected me with the person. I know what you're thinking. How did it go?

It wasn't as great as it would have been for a Doer, but clients and archetypes differ. Still, instead of a client that would ghost me, I got to work with the integrator in his team, and we got the things installed in their Fulfillment Funnel that would make the biggest impact. The results showed in just a couple of weeks!.

Later, the owner shared with me how much their dropout rate had reduced and how confident they were in scaling this offer.

Do It Yourself

This exercise is a continuation of the one you started in the introduction of the archetypes chapter. You can go deeper now that you know more about how Worriers are wired.

Please use this worksheet so you can review this chapter yourself and use your takeaways to apply this to your business and offers.

Click or go to the website: https://ethicalscaling.com/csm-book-downloads/

Scan me to download

Start by going through your client roster:

- Now that you have a client roster labeled with archetypes, identify the Worriers.

- Check if the majority got great results while working with you.

- Also, check how many of them were renewed or upgraded to a different offer.

- Check if you got drop-outs or refunds from any Worrier.

- Equipped with the knowledge you have now, what would you do differently in the future when working with a

Worrier?

Worriers can use up a lot of the fulfillment team's time, so being prepared in advance will help reduce waste and inefficiency in your Fulfillment Funnel.

Takeaways

I'd risk saying this archetype is the most common within the lower levels of Maslow's Pyramid, so it is a big part of the marketplace in many offers. Worriers struggle with safety so providing a safe environment for them is essential.

Worriers, but also Followers, can suffer from the same problems, they struggle with action, and the difference between knowing what to do and doing is based on the motivation to act.

Learning to manage them will give you a broader impact opportunity and create raving fans like never before.

Summary:

- Craves novelty and gets a lot of hope from new shiny things.

- Leads their life on quick bursts of excitement.

- Has a craving for attention and neediness.

- Typically has a lot of questions.

- Gets easily overwhelmed.

- Permission-based feedback works great.

What if a client is more emotionally or empathy-based and not a Worrier? Well, you just described a Follower.

Vd. FOLLOWER

Never Gets Better

"The meme for blind faith secures its perpetuation by the simple unconscious expedient of discouraging rational inquiry."

Richard Dawkins

The land of the Blind

Long ago, five older men lived in a village in Africa. Each was born blind. Everyone made sure to take care of them and protect them from things they couldn't defend themselves against.

Although they were born with no vision, they were very curious and had tons of imagination. One of the things they were more curious about was Elephants. They heard elephants were strong, could carry lots of weight on their back, and could be louder than a storm.

They had this insatiable curiosity about elephants, and they dreamed of having the opportunity to find one. One day, one of the villagers shared that he had a daughter who owned an elephant, and he asked if the elders would like to visit and meet the elephant, which they all accepted on the spot.

When the blind men met the elephant, each of them went to touch the creature and have this incredible experience they were looking for. It finally happened!

The first blind man, after touching the side of the creature, said it didn't feel like a creature but like a wall made of stone.

The second blind man, after touching the creature's tail, said it felt like a snake.

The third blind man touched the elephant's tusk and said that the creature felt like a deadly spear.

The fourth blind man, after touching one of the elephant's legs, said it felt like a giant cow.

The fifth blind man, after touching the elephant's ear, said it couldn't be a creature but a carpet that could fly over the mountains.

The five blind men were confused as they all perceived the creature differently.

They shouted, "wall, snake, spear, cow, carpet!"

Until a very wise man arrived and asked the elders to calm down. After a couple of deep breaths, the wise man said:

"This creature is an enormous animal. Each of you has touched only one part, but if you put the parts together, you'll see the truth."

Followers sometimes follow blindly, without thinking about connecting the dots or finding the truth. They will blindly trust another blind man who touched only one part of the elephant.

This is why this is one of my favorite sayings:

In the land of the blind, the one-eyed man is king.

You can feel like a king when dealing with Followers, but that doesn't provide them with what they need. It will only reinforce the idea of them being "blind" followers. They'll stay where they have always been, stuck.

Serving a Follower

This archetype is tricky. His attitude is entirely different from all the others.

Followers don't bother to push to new levels that could allow them to be better and have the life they truly desire. As soon as they can be average and be seen by others as "normal," they will settle. They prefer the certainty of misery to the misery of uncertainty as Virginia Satir says.

The Follower lives a life of complacency, accepting the status quo and what society says is correct as the only way to live their life. Internally, they have an overwhelming inferiority complex that doesn't necessarily make them feel bad or angry but shows up in their complacency and the lack of necessary action.

Followers tend to be friendly, so they trust that others have their best interests in mind. This makes them an easy-to-please archetype, and they'll give you signals that they're bought in on the process, even when they're not. They're just being nice.

Because they lead more with emotion than logic, they'll connect with the ideas and goals you discuss with them. The main problem is that they're so in their head, so focused on the talking, that they end up taking little to no action. On top of that, because they don't love numbers, asking them to track something is almost impossible. This creates headaches as you want to know how much is getting done.

Interestingly, some of these clients will be happy working with you even when they don't get great results because they judge the experience more on how they feel than the results you help them achieve.

This might sound like a good idea, but it's shortsighted. Yes, it's better for them to be happy with your cheerleading than not, but at the same time, if they don't get results, it's almost impossible for them to stay part of your bow-tie funnel. They won't ascend and buy from you again.

Please, don't throw in the towel yet. You can serve these clients well.

Although they don't love numbers, you can always find common ground on something that doesn't turn them off and gives you enough information to be precise with your diagnosis. For Followers using the "doctor" frame, and asking them to bring enough information to help you diagnose and prescribe like a doctor, can get them to embrace change.

But more importantly, check how this archetype feels throughout the process to understand if the expectations on both ends are clear and ensure communication is aligned.

Followers are the archetype that will benefit from simplicity the most, so please don't overcomplicate and help them take action!

Flipping the Script for a Follower

When they feel they're not seen or heard, Followers can go to either Victim or Persecutor.

If you feel your Follower client is showing up like a Persecutor, please refer to the section on Flipping the Script for a Controller. If you think their frame of mind is a Victim, please refer to the Flipping the Script for a Worrier section.

Here is a simple guide to serving this archetype well:

- Be systematic and objective.

- Be consistent with your feedback and answer the <u>why</u> (a deeper reason for action).

- Clearly define what you want from them (they'll want to please you).

- Be patient.

- Ask <u>how</u> questions (this helps their brain focus on solutions and picturing the work).

Remember that Followers can go deep into a sense of an obsessive inferiority complex which can make them lack so much self-confidence that they stay frozen and lack the power to act.

Serving a Follower Clinic

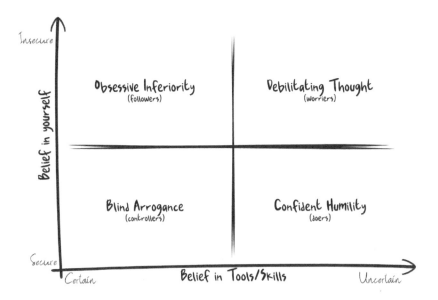

I'll share a fascinating client story of an experience I had recently. This client was considered by me to be a Follower since we started our work with him, but I had the gut feeling that if we doubled down on his self-confidence, he'd be one of the most incredible success stories we had worked with. I'm happy that I had the right gut feeling.

We started working together, and he wasn't our perfect client revenue-wise. He was a little under what we look for in clients regarding team size, revenue, and client roster. But he was on the right trajectory and showed some success and ethics.

Maybe due to some old experiences, he didn't see the same possibilities I saw for him. So belief in himself was a big lever here.

As a Follower, inevitably, he was attracting a lot of Followers as clients. Equipped with this information, I worked on getting some quick wins, reassuring him he was on the right track and giving him bite-sized action plans that could be implemented immediately.

We met a bit more often than we typically do with other archetypes, but I knew investing in this client would be worth it.

The results were staggering. They went from high churn within the first six weeks of working together to zero churn.

They went from no backend offer to creating one that was sold out immediately, generating more than 6 figures in revenue.

The team was able to handle more clients and I trained them to help them effectively guide clients so that the owner could enjoy his freedom and his dream of working from anywhere in the world while having multiple vacations a year.

Interestingly, after six months of working together, they had a record month where they tripled their revenue while the owner was on a 3 week vacation. They hadn't increased ad spend, or any other acquisition costs, but their monthly recurring revenue was up; they benefited from no churn and started the referral request process.

They deserve all the credit, and when I look at the owner I don't see a Follower anymore. We have a brand new Doer in the house that will make lots of noise in his industry.

Do It Yourself

This exercise is a continuation of the one you started in the introduction of the archetypes chapter. You can do deeper now that you know more about how Followers are wired.

Please use this worksheet so you can review this chapter yourself and use your takeaways to apply this to your business and offers.

Click or go to the website: https://ethicalscaling.com/csm-book-downloads/

Scan me to download

Start by going through your client roster:

- Now that you have a client roster labeled with archetypes, identify the Followers.

- Check if the majority got great results while working with you.

- Also, check how many of them were renewed or upgraded to a different offer.

- Check if you got drop-outs or refunds from any Followers.

- Equipped with the knowledge you have now, what would you do differently in the future when working with a Follower?

Followers lack implementation; they just want to "be". If we can identify them early enough and nudge them forward, they can be great clients.

Takeaways

Personally, I find Followers harder to manage as they can be frustrating to work with.

Sometimes with Followers, due to their complacency, you can benefit from creating a crisis to convince them they could be facing a catastrophe and have no choice but to move.

I believe that we can achieve everything in life, so for me, it's hard to understand how someone can have such a feeling of inferiority. But, I got some coaching to learn how to guide this archetype.

Summary:

- They have different attitudes than the other archetypes;

they feel easy to guide.

- Complacent and accepts being average.

- Typically nice people to chat with.

- Wants to feel seen and heard.

- Needs to get in action, or it's a never-ending plateau story.

Is this it? Are we done yet? No, not yet.

It's time to connect the dots, and we want to help you end the book with an Action Plan and also give you some bonuses. Are you ready?

VI. APPLICATION

"Too often, we convince ourselves that massive results require massive action."

James Clear

Wanna Jam with us?

Imagine you go to a food store, one of those fancy gourmet ones.

When you walk in you find a table full of imported jams that you can try for free. Who doesn't love free food?

You go there on day one and there are 6 different jams to try.

You go there the day after, and now there are 24 jams to try.

Day two attracted many people to the tasting table. And you started thinking: "this tasting approach is such a success," until you find out people weren't buying the day two options at all. You find out that people that went there on day one and saw only 6 jams were 10 times more likely to buy a jar of jam.

Wow, surprising. What happened was decision paralysis. When you have more options, even good ones, it can make you freeze. At the end of the day, having a book full of choices could be debilitating.

And I know that you, my friend, like any of the archetypes described in this book have: a Rider, an Elephant, and a Journey ahead of you. Our goal in writing this book is to give you direction on how to use these tools as soon as you finish reading each chapter.

I want to reduce the number of choices you have to make so your Rider's life is easier. So we will save your mental bandwidth for what matters: keeping your business running smoothly and enjoying your life.

Assuming, by now, I've got your Elephant to be completely bought-in in seeing customer success as the way to build a sustainable business. Next I'll address your Rider.

After reading the book, you'll have to decide what to implement, and I want to avoid your Rider getting exhausted.

It can be challenging to think you'll change how you've been doing things for the past several months or years. This will create uncertainty.

The way forward is to go through the Application scenarios in this chapter, and if you have the time, I highly recommend going through the Bonus Section as well.

In this chapter, you'll find clear directions on implementing all of what we talked about for every client archetype.

We aim not to give you a rigid plan that you must follow verbatim, like a script. That's not our style. We know you want to control how things are done, so we will give you the most important pieces you need to get your Fulfillment Funnel running smoothly.

We will focus on the critical pieces that can change your business to create great Relationships at Scale.

How can you use Archetypes?

When you look back at the four typical archetypes, know that they are not perfect or set in stone, but having these containers and buckets will help you think and label people and understand how you can best help them.

If you look inside yourself, you could be a Worrier for some parts of your life, a Controller in others, and even a Follower in others!

Whatever the scenario is, there is always space to become a Doer. And that's the path to great fulfillment when you understand the long-term effects of Relationships at Scale.

This goes against how our minds work nowadays. When you can

order a Big Mac to be at your door without even taking off your slippers, where your favorite online streaming software starts the next episode automatically... We're creating a self-fulfilling prophecy that any pain and plateaus can and should be avoided.

We believe that symptoms can be treated in minutes, but the real problem lasts your whole life. You might be treating your lack of client results or retention the same way.

The society we live in today only cares about results, not the process, and it is reflected in what you see all around you. More drug usage, more overweight people, more people with bad debt, and more people living la "Vida Loca".

We're losing the gift of patience and dedication. But not you. You can find your path and help others do the same. We can all become great Doers.

Your main goal while using the Archetype framework is to take ownership of your own life and help your clients do the same. And if you don't have clarity on what you want, you're taking the risk of the misery of certainty.

Progress is based on brief moments of improvement followed by long periods of work where you feel no progress. But the frequency and repetition of daily practices will build your progress long-term and will compound over time. Isn't that the 8th wonder of the world, like Einstein said?

And between us, you just need the intention to get it done, knowing exactly what's in it for you. When using the Archetypes with clients, your primary goal is to help them:

- Practice deliberately.

- Get better at honing the skills that will get them closer to their goals.

- Challenge them to aim for higher levels of competence.

- Help them accept living most of their time on a plateau before a growth spurt.

- Plant seeds for the love of practice, even when they don't see any measurable progress.

Even when no progress is measurable, you're transforming your behaviors into new habits that will happen on auto-pilot later. The learning phase is happening even when you don't notice it. And the work is never wasted. It's accumulated. Look back at the chapter about understanding motivation, and you will see that there is a great valley of despair that makes clients feel like nothing is happening like they dreamed it would.

You'll become a leader by helping your clients integrate this framework into their life. Everyone craves someone to lead, not to please. You and your team can be those leaders.

Applying this book's concepts to different archetypes

Gradual and Consistent Improvement

A. Doers

Big Outcome

Doers have big dreams, and they typically have achieved a lot in life. That being said, they will prefer things that help with tangible results, like conserving time and money, making more money, or improving their status.

This is not one-size-fits-all solution, but a good line of thought on how you can use some of the previous concepts, I've shared, immediately.

Can you predict when Doers will achieve a tangible milestone that makes them feel empowered to continue?

Perceived Likelihood of Achievement

Doers tend to easily trust themselves, so it's more about the belief around the offer and the process you have in place for them.

If you can be present, guide them and support them, this part of the offer is easy to tackle.

Time Delay

Doers tend to be excited about new processes and discoveries, so they'll be more willing to wait to get where they want to be.

Making sure the process is fast enough for their taste is essential, but more than that, ensuring they feel like they're getting there is priority.

Are you checking in with them to see their progress? Are you facilitating a feedback loop?

Effort

Normally, high-performers by default, effort doesn't feel daunting for Doers, so it's not about how much effort they need to put in but more about how that effort connects to what they want.

If working more gives them the status they want, they will without blinking an eye.

Fulfillment Continuum

As I said, Doers trust themselves a lot, so when you think about buyer's remorse for Doers, it's only applicable when you drop the ball. If you get Doers dropping out, go immediately to the drawing board and understand the gap between sales, fulfillment, and the onboarding process that's turning them off.

If you connect with them and provide clarity, they're bought in. You'll see some more examples in the following chapter called "Bonus Section".

Expectation Management

Although effort is not a problem, per se, for Doers, it's always essential to have the right expectations. One of the risks you can face if you don't do proper expectation management is to get a Doer to behave like a Controller and burn himself out.

Find what timeline makes sense for them based on a sustainable level of effort, and keep reviewing that periodically.

Buy-in Framework in action

- The Emotion
- The Logic
- The Pathway

As Doers tend to be in the more Logical bucket, you can adjust your efforts when building a relationship with them.

Focusing a little more on logic and how to give them clarity on the next steps while connecting the dots between the task at hand and the future tasks and milestones will get Doers to buy-in in no time.

Obsessively from bump to bump

B. Controllers

Big Outcome

Regarding the Big Outcome, Controllers are similar to Doers; they have typically had some success in the past, so they understand that dreaming big is possible. They will prefer things like conserving time and money, making more money, or improving their status.

Perceived Likelihood of Achievement

Controllers tend to have an easy time trusting themselves like Doers. Still, Controllers have serious trust issues, so they'll measure your confidence level to analyze how trustworthy the process is.

If you have solid boundaries and show up confident but humble to know you don't know everything, you'll find them more open to accepting the goal and the process.

Time Delay

Controllers have many similarities to Doers, but they tend to be more obsessive and rushed, making them prone to errors in their decision-making process.

This can make them more impatient than Doers, as they'll be second-guessing what you tell them to do.

For Controllers, giving them a quick win and an epiphany around how things can and should be done will build trust and thus reduce time delay.

Effort

Controllers, much like Doers, are high-performers by default. The effort is typically not the issue, but applying it to the right things can be.

They might try to push your team and change the process, they might end up in a rabbit hole doing more than they should, only to free fall off a cliff.

Redirecting and challenging them in non-conflicting ways will get them to stay the course and apply the right effort to the right things.

Fulfillment Continuum

I said this previously, the Controller has trust issues. So it's not an easy job to get them to be completely bought in.

It's essential to gauge how trustworthy they feel like you are during their early interactions to make sure they resonate with what you do and how you do it.

Clarity and self-confidence will be the key ingredients to move them to buy-in on the continuum.

Expectation Management

The biggest challenge for Controllers is their ability to put in effort while having very high expectations.

This tendency to be obsessed with goals can make them go too fast with little results to show, making them perceive the work as valueless.

We want the offer to be perceived as highly valuable, and a simple strategy for this archetype could be to not spend much time challenging them on timelines but challenge them a bit more on their Big Outcome and Aspirational identity.

We know this archetype is always in a rush, so we can try to help them understand the side effects of sustaining a crazy level of effort just to make things happen a bit faster. We're teaching patience.

Remember that Controllers are the ones that believe that one woman can give birth to a baby in 9 months, but 9 women together will be able to give birth in 1 month. Overly logical, they can lose touch with reality.

Buy-in Framework in action

- The Emotion

- The Logic

- The Pathway

Controllers tend to be in the more Logical bucket, so we can adjust our efforts when building a relationship with them.

Focusing a little more on logic and how to give them clarity on the next steps, and managing their obsessiveness with the goals being achieved, can give you the best path forward for them.

Also, this archetype benefits from Clarity and Direction, giving them an attractive Big Outcome (destination) and more flexibility to figure out the "how." You give them the "recipe for success," but you let them figure out a little of the in-betweens so they don't feel micromanaged.

This is just how they're wired. This archetype loves analyzing, which puts them in a tough spot. They spend more time thinking than taking action because of trust issues around your offer's process. Let them figure out some of the in-betweens; let them Control.

I'm also going to give you another concept to keep in mind, that can work wonders for Controllers, Worriers and Followers.

We've discussed that buy-in could be challenging for Controllers that struggle with trust issues or for Worriers and Followers who struggle with trusting themselves.

For these three archetypes, you need to work around trusting yourself and/or your process.

One concept I love, from the book *Switch* by Chip and Dan Heath, is the concept of shrinking change to build trust.

One way to get people moving is to have them climb a hill before climbing the mountain. After climbing the hill, showing them the progress will build trust in what has been done.

Another way to escalate their commitment is through a quick start, which gets them more bought-in. Let's look at a study done about this.

In this study, when people were told they needed 10 stamps on their car wash loyalty cards to get a free wash, only 19% completed their card. In a variation of this, another group was told they needed 12 stamps instead of 10, and they were delivered a card that already had 2 stamps on it. The funny thing was that now 34% completed the card; we're talking about almost double the number of people for the same effort.

Giving archetypes tiny action plans that will lead them to the milestones they want to achieve makes easy wins even easier.

Keep in mind that for Controllers, this will lead them to trust the process more, and for Worriers and Followers, this helps them build trust in themselves. Win-win.

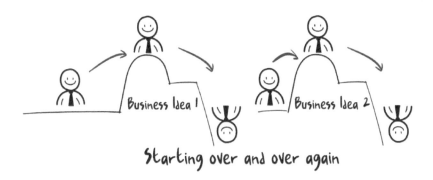

Starting over and over again

C. Worriers

Big Outcome

Regarding the Big Outcome, Worriers fall under a different umbrella. Yes, making money, status, and other resources can be relevant, but they tend to be more concerned about belonging to social networks, they desire meaning, and most want to be generous and help others live a good life.

Can you connect that big Aspirational identity with what you're doing with them while you work together?

Perceived Likelihood of Achievement

As Worriers tend to get overwhelmed easily and jump from one thing to another, building their actions on top of excitement only, they are never able to build a strong belief in themselves.

Helping them take action and creating confidence will ensure this part is tackled and out of sight.

On top of that, as they tend to be suspicious about big promises, make sure they trust you while giving them plenty of honest reassurance.

Remember not to save them or fall prey to creating codependency, as it only provides a self-fulfilling prophecy that they can't do it themselves.

Time Delay

Worriers are interesting because they get overwhelmed quite quickly and tolerate little effort due to already being exhausted and always in a rush.

You'll be dealing with various challenges with this archetype, so you need to ensure things are addressed as early as possible.

Giving them bite-sized action plans will help with the overwhelm. Understanding what's a realistic effort level for them will give them a sense of control. And making sure they can zoom out so they can keep their anxiety in check.

Effort

As I said in the Time Delay, they tolerate less information than logical archetypes, and they're already tired, probably from trying too many things.

With that in mind, an effort that is sustainable for days or weeks is what they need in order to trust themselves more and tackle more significant challenges.

Fulfillment Continuum

As Worriers are always looking for an excuse or validation around their beliefs about something not working for them, these are the clients that will do their best to stay stuck in a buyer's remorse stage.

Building that confidence in themselves and the process will make them more committed and in action.

Expectation Management

The biggest challenge for Worriers is the mismatch between very high expectations and unwillingness or ability to put in enough effort. But because they're so burned out, they still perceive that they're doing their best.

If you want to avoid them jumping from our solution to another, you need to address this as early as possible to help them trip over the truth.

Most Worriers will accept a longer timeline if they see the light at the end of the tunnel and if this allows them to put in little effort.

They're willing to accept the compromise if they feel as though it's for their own good.

Buy-in Framework in action

- The Emotion

- The Logic

- The Pathway

Worriers tend to be in the more Emotional bucket, so it's useful to keep that in mind when building a relationship with them.

Focusing a little more on Emotions can go a long way, which will help you uncover their core motivators and connect with them to make them more willing to embrace change.

Remember that Worriers are terrific at staying stuck inside their heads; after spinning their wheels, they overanalyze everything without doing anything. Also, on top of that, the analysis is only problem-focused. They end up being obsessed with problems instead of solutions.

Never Gets Better

D. Followers

Big Outcome

Regarding the Big Outcome, Followers go with Worriers under the emotional umbrella. They desire meaning, and most want to be generous and help others live good lives.

Perceived Likelihood of Achievement

As Followers tend to follow and not be overly excited about an end goal, they try a little and accept little results as a byproduct.

This doesn't damage any belief around the outcome or offer but reinforces their idea that it works for others but not for them.

More than Worriers, Followers need to take lots of bite-sized action early on to help them follow through, which is what they struggle with the most.

As Followers typically never had big dreams or goals, they can feel less excited about tangible things, making them believe it's not worth it.

Time Delay

Followers are curious and one of a kind because they'll not feel anxious or overwhelmed even if you give them a lot to do because it doesn't matter subconsciously. They're not planning on putting a lot of action into it.

This can create confusion for the person dealing with them, as it feels like they say yes to anything just to show up without anything done.

If for any reason, you catch this early, you should make sure you reduce the workload and add extra accountability that will work as a feedback loop.

This will give them some momentum, and the feedback will make them believe it's worth it.

Effort

As I said in Time Delay, they tolerate less information than logical archetypes, and they're already doing many things that don't add value to their goals.

With that in mind, an effort that is sustainable for days or weeks is what they need to trust themselves more and tackle bigger challenges.

Fulfillment Continuum

Followers are never super excited about anything unless we give them a kickstart that can change how they act, they'll spend the whole time stuck, and I know this can be nerve-wracking.

This doesn't necessarily mean they'll feel buyer's remorse, but it won't help them be completely bought in.

The fastest way to get them bought in is to get them to take action.

Expectation Management

The biggest challenge for Followers is low expectations, accepting timelines that are too long, and putting in little to no effort.

They need a different approach than Worriers. They need to be challenged to live the Big Outcome and Aspirational Identity. It must excite them and ignite that fire to help them take action.

This will help them move from milestone to milestone until they understand they're getting closer to their goal.

Most Followers won't love the idea of putting in more effort, but they'll accept the idea of having bigger goals that can get them to live the life they want.

Buy-in Framework in action

- The Emotion

- The Logic

- The Pathway

Focusing a little more on Emotions can go a long way, which will help us uncover their core motivators and connect with them to make them more willing to embrace change.

Remember that Followers are astute and logically understand what you want them to do, but they're dealing with an internal battle between logic and emotion. To get them motivated to act, the Elephant needs to be engaged.

For some clients, this could mean the appeal of a desire, like the Aspirational Identity we discussed before, or it can also be something harmful, like loss aversion. What are they afraid to lose?

Negative emotions can work in moments when the Elephant is stuck and can bring a sense of urgency when people get too comfortable, like the typical complacent nature of a Follower.

Takeaways

Working with clients is interesting. As long as you do business in the Human to Human niche, you'll benefit from Relationships at Scale, and loyalty will pay off.

Let's quickly review this chapter.

Summary:

- Avoid analysis paralysis like in the Jam experiment.

- Remember the four ingredients of high LTV offers will resonate differently with the four archetypes.

- Moving away from buyer's remorse is one of the biggest priorities.

- Expectation management helps build the client's responsibility.

- Buy-in connects all parts of our brain for a coherent process.

Before you close the book and never open it again, I just want you to be aware of some traps you could find when wanting to implement this. Also, in the bonus section, you can check some examples of how to apply these concepts from work we've done with our consulting clients that you can easily use as a swipe file.

Traps when implementing the strategies and tactics in this book

Let's keep a few things in mind when applying the Archetype framework.

A. Status Quo

Status quo is a fancy name for what we call equilibrium. Everything in your body and mind tries to work with a balance or homeostasis.

While equilibrium saves time and energy, it can also be inertia when you're trying to achieve the next level of personal growth; it's the resistance to change, confirming what you have, sometimes to a level of complacency.

Equilibrium is not good or bad. It's just how we find stability amidst the chaos.

Anytime you start something new, you'll feel the urge to return to old habits, but please don't panic. That is good news. It means you're doing something different and that you're changing.

You're getting ready for a growth phase, and your body and mind are fighting the new balance. And your client, independent of the archetype, will feel the same.

B. Process Flexibility

There are two extremes:

- Quit anytime it gets tricky like a Worrier

- Or try harder like a Controller

The resistance you feel is proportional to the size and speed of the change you're trying to implement. This is why I believe the way forward might include baby steps one after the other instead of overwhelming long and challenging action plans.

In a moment of immense inertia, you can always negotiate a pause or a little step back so you can recover and then build momentum again.

The main message is that you'll get it done if you keep alert for the symptoms and are flexible in negotiating timelines and milestones. Remember, at the end of the day, your clients are not you. But even you can fall prey to fatigue and fall back to the path of least resistance.

As I explained in the Fulfillment Continuum chapter, being available to have an expectation conversation can be massive for client leadership.

Apply the same concepts to your own expectations about what will happen after implementing the strategies in this book. Review your timelines and the effort available for its implementation.

C. Feedback Loops

Help them learn how to practice the new skills and how they can do them not just for the result but for the sake of practice. When the process becomes enjoyable, and you disconnect from the results, you build a long-term habit and sustainable change.

The funny thing is that when the practice becomes a habit, the results will come even if you don't think about them. From now on, you don't practice. **You're practicing**.

Building a great fulfillment funnel and process is not the goal; the customer-centric approach to your offers is.

D. Ultimate Goal

"Knowledge takes no space."

Learning is changing, and change is good. Life is not a weekend, and this is why studying without implementation feels worthless.

Humans are one of a kind and the only animal in nature that has evolved at this speed to the level where we are today. Knowing that, when you learn something new that's not in your genes, like the Customer Manifesto Frameworks, it's one of the skills that can set you apart. But it needs to be embodied through implementation.

And now you ask, *"how long will it take?"*

I'll use George Leonard's words: *"How long will you live?"*

Becoming an Ideal Customer Engineer, using archetypes and coaching skills, and integrating all the Fulfillment Continuum ideas, is not an event. It's an ongoing process.

The same applies to your clients. If they understand that, they'll stay for life. Why wouldn't they?

Last note

Remember that this is just a starting point when going through this real transformation.

This book builds a transformational framework: what to look for, implementation examples, and a filter for what needs to be done.

The goal is not to have a perfect plan of action to get you to the result you want.

Yes, there is some guidance in this book on implementing some low-hanging fruit plans of action, but keep two things in mind: where you're starting and where you want to go.

Forget about the middle because the middle will be different once you're there, and the book will have the tools to adapt to where you are. Also, think about who could be on board in this process for change with you, someone that is different and can bring perspective.

Ben and I are wired very differently, and embracing that has put us here today. I want to give you a little more perspective on how partnering up can work well when we understand each other.

I know I could be a great CEO, but I don't feel that's my genius.

When Ben launched one of his first offers, *The Empowered CEO*, I saw him doing stuff that was mind-blowing with owners.

And instead of allowing my ego to get in the way, I embraced my genius, and Ben embraced his. Knowing our strengths and weaknesses made us stronger and helped build our brand.

Although Ben is a great CEO, I can still be a great addition:

- I'm great with Operations after being a Systems Engineer for ten years and managing a team under the ops department.

- I'm able to bring great perspectives and experience across several industries.

- I have some counterintuitive approaches and a different thought process.

What did Ben bring that makes him so special and a critical piece in our consulting business? He is great at making decisions. This makes us a great team.

On the other hand, I'm fascinated with psychology, and our end goal as a company is to take our mission further. And we're at a place in our lives where being true to ourselves is one of the most important things.

We both know we would never be able to help all the service-based businesses out there, but we can give them this book which will work wonders while implementing by themselves.

Now that you understand our synergy as a Team, you can understand why I say Ben should be called The Soul if some of our clients call me The Brain. And this is why we feel so good about giving value away without expecting anything in return.

Yes, I know, a long journey starts with a single step, but a single action doesn't guarantee a long journey. My goal is to keep you going. And remember, change is not an event. It'll be a process. A customer-centric and profitable process.

And when this change happens for good, it follows a pattern: where the direction is clear, motivation is high, and the environment is supportive. You got this.

But if you feel overseeing your customer success department is not your wheelhouse, reach out to us. Let's figure out if we can train your team, help you find talent, or even run your team for you. As you know, we're not into just pitching people; we love relationships and would love to connect with you.

Just remember this: if your clients leave your business feeling worse than when they started, there is something that can still be done. *Ethical Scaling is the way.*

To a path of outstanding business and personal fulfillment,

Jay and Ben

VII. BONUS SECTION

"People will forget what you said, people will forget what you did, but people will never forget how you made them feel. "

Maya Angelou

Why this section is 100% free

We feel we have made the book pretty good so far and that you have plenty of ideas, frameworks, strategies, tactics, and other things to work with. But we didn't want to stop there.

We wanted to add a Bonus Section to kick things up a notch. But why?

Like I often say, I love inception.

People feel a rush of positive energy when you offer a free thing or bonus, but free things can also make people act irrationally. I can share two quick examples with you.

An experiment was run at Costco, where they were giving free samples:

- In 2015, a 78-year-old was punched in the face after a 24-year-old accused him of grabbing too many Nutella waffle samples.

- In 2018, two customers slapped each other in the face while waiting for cheeseburger samples.

Funny how people can go crazy for a little sample or bonus. It channels desire but also brings some of our irrationality to the surface, as Dan Ariely would say.

One of Dan's studies asked someone to go to a party and offer free tattoos, and he found out that even when people didn't want to get inked, they now wanted it because it was free.

This is why this bonus is free. It would be best if you didn't think we created all the ideas in the book so that you now have no choice but to hire us. That's not the goal.

The bonus section will be the cherry on top. All the concepts we've discussed applied to all the areas we explore when working with our consulting clients, from the Optimized Journey, Team Optimizer, and the Profit Multiplier.

How to apply this to have a Raving Fan Business

Ben and I feel like most books, courses, and training out there focus solely on theory and lack the implementation guidance to get people to win. We want to stand out in a way that helps your Ideal Customer Engineers to be the best by applying what we provide in this book.

Remember that all you have learned so far can be applied across several areas of your business including: offers, team and interactions with clients.

Clients will want to feel that the experience is delightful, that their worldviews are changing, that they're at their best, and that they can see others going through the same while following the path.

Let's go through a couple of examples of how you can implement them in practice for your business.

Bring your clients closer to their Aspirational Identity

James March from Stanford University says that, as humans, we have two kinds of choices:

1. Consequences: it's the typical economic approach based on cost-benefits. It's rational and analytical.

2. Identity: it's based on who you perceive yourself to be.

    o   Who am I?

- ○ What situation is this?

- ○ What would someone like me do in this situation?

The latter explains why parents make sacrifices without seeing an excellent cost-benefit. It's based on their Identity.

And this Identity is not born in us. It's adopted through life. And when a client purchases your offer, they have hope it will get them closer to their Aspirational Identity.

Imagine my story; I joined a high-ticket mastermind a few years ago, and if I think about that decision today through a consequences-only lens. It was the worst decision ever.

But based on my Identity, I'd have done that again, over and over. It helped me become who I am and spend time with people I want to hang out with. On purpose or not, that experience shaped my decision-making process to be more aligned with my new Identity.

Can you help your clients feel the same Identity growth?

Sales Calls

The journey starts before your client gets to your fulfillment team. The sales call is an excellent opportunity to explore the Aspirational Identity and engineer Hope which drives the Belief that the goal can happen.

After consulting with more than 100 hundred 7 and 8-figure businesses, one of the biggest problems is the handoff process between the Sales and the Fulfillment departments.

First, the Sales Rep rarely sees the whole Bow-tie funnel, so they focus on the acquisition funnel and closing the client. This is very ineffective as we leave a lot of money on the table because the clients are unaware of a possible long-term journey.

Secondly, the typical sales process focuses on the top part of the High LTV offer equation, the Big Outcome and Perceived Likelihood of Achievement. This information should be shared as notes with the fulfillment team immediately so that they have as much information as possible to show your clients you have internal team cohesiveness when you first interact with them.

Third, Sales Reps should have a fair idea of what archetypes are. Not to the level of your Ideal Customer Engineers, but at least a hint of what they might be. As I said, I can be a Controller on a sales call but a Doer when doing the work. If the sales rep feels like I'm acting based on a lack of trust on the sales call, that information should be shared with fulfillment to ensure they address the belief asap. This will apply to any archetype. It will give the fulfillment team direction on where to focus.

Fourth, if you think about the Fulfillment Continuum, the moment after the sale is probably the one with the higher potential to be skewed to the left and where buyer's remorse can be high. A straightforward solution is to bridge the gap with an excellent welcome process.

Welcome

The Welcome process is the next point after the sale and should happen as fast as possible.

How we do it is less relevant, it could be a call, an email, an SMS, or any other medium of exchange. It is essential to mark this transition moment and to confirm the client's decision to work with you was the right one. This is the moment when the buy-in process starts.

If you have a typical Big Outcome, make sure you reinforce that Aspirational Identity in your initial welcome process, reminding them why they pulled the trigger.

Reinforcing the belief that this is the right thing for them can keep them on track before you officially onboard them to fully benefit from your offerings.

Onboarding

I want to share another story from my engineering days. I arrived at work on the first day. I showed up, and the receptionist who was there didn't even know who I was, or she wasn't expecting me.

She guided me to a desk with a monitor and phone, but there was no computer there and nothing to do. Also, my new boss wasn't available either, but they gave me their HR guidebook to read.

This lack of attention was overwhelming, and I've seen people in the online service business falling prey to the same, which is disappointing. The onboarding process doesn't need to be crazy, but it needs to create that transition moment where your client understands they're starting something new, something that's worthwhile.

Remembering that your clients want that Aspirational Identity, this is the opportunity to mark that the Identity is changing. It's an *old you vs. new you* experience.

During this onboarding process, you want to create that feeling of certainty like Uber did when adding the map to their app. It's that certainty and predictability that allows you to paint a journey with all the touchpoints around inflection points.

In our experience, you can decide to eliminate any call from your service except the onboarding call, based on exactly what I said above. It's such an excellent opportunity to create high LTV.

Let's look more closely at the specific ideas in this book and how to apply them.

First, the Onboarding process is the perfect opportunity to explore the bottom part of the High LTV offer equation. It allows you to discuss time and effort, creating appropriate expectations.

Secondly, you can start the buy-in process immediately to understand the tangible thing they want, the aspirational thing that gets their emotions to be motivated, and how you can shape the path ahead of them.

Third, most clients will show who they are archetype-wise in this call, so if you don't have any previous info on how to label them, you should start here. This will help you tailor your communication moving forward.

I want your clients to have the opposite experience I had as an engineer. Sadly my bad experience continued, and I was left staring at a wall for a couple of weeks. I found my way to success, but most people would have resigned. That's what you will avoid with a great onboarding process.

1:1 Interactions with clients

Your service will have 1:1 interactions with clients, but they won't all be 1:1 calls.

A service will have some synchronous and asynchronous communication and probably, a mix of both. Those interactions, which we usually refer to as touchpoints, are an excellent opportunity to create relationships at scale and deepen those relationships. This is the time to use the archetypes framework.

One of your biggest levers is expectation management. Any interaction is an opportunity to remind clients of the expectation, the Big Outcome they're looking for, and how important it is.

Remember that there are four things clients want:

1. **Easy Like a Piece of Cake**: If working with you is easy, they don't need more 1:1 interactions to get unstuck. Make your offer a guided self-service experience.

2. **Next Issue Avoidance**: When clients need to interact 1:1 with you a lot, don't focus solely on the problem they have now. Take the time to address the next issues they will have and normalize them.

3. **Empathy**: Succeeding on the emotional side of the interaction with clients will be transformational; this is what we call Experience Engineering.

4. **Empower Teams**: If you have employees, empower them to make the client's life easier, and reduce effort whenever possible. Reward your team for doing that.

There are at least three big synchronous touchpoints that will optimize these 1:1 interactions with clients:

1. Onboarding.

2. 14 to 30-day check-in.

3. The Perfect Last Touchpoint.

I'll describe these three in a second, but there are other types of asynchronous touchpoints:

- Manual: Normally, when tracking a client's progress, we will know when to reach out and how to assess their engagement, commitment, and buy-in to prevent any regret or drop-out.

- Automated: this could be preplanned for a journey where we know the times for the inflection points, and we can create an automatic trigger.

I know most people will look for automated approaches, but my experience says those are less relevant and have less impact on the relationship with the client. I'd avoid them and make sure we focus on the others.

14 to 30-day check-in

Your clients can be more prone to buyer's remorse during the first couple of weeks of working with you. It will be wise to plan some check-ins (manual, sync or async, or even automated) during this period to prevent them from dropping out.

In my opinion, this is the perfect opportunity to increase your LTV with a concise and to-the-point call. But that's just our preference.

Here are some simple things that help create respect and trust around what you're doing with them:

- Remind them of the Big Outcome and find out if they still connect with the Aspirational Identity to avoid Outcome Regret.

- Go through their initial expectations, review the effort needed to reach the goal in the agreed upon timeline, and find where they are in the journey.

- If the results are slower than what you or they thought they would be, this is a great opportunity to provide leadership and discuss why (diagnose).

- Explain that you have high standards and expectations for them but let them select their own pace: if they want to push harder or take a bit longer to be where they want to be, you will let them decide and hold them accountable.

- After you let them decide their own pace, you can plant the seeds for what might be coming next: either a continuation if they need a longer timeline or another offer after they finish this one.

The Perfect Last Touchpoint

What are the main goals of the Perfect Last Touchpoint:

- Leave your clients wanting more.

- Give them a memorable ending.

- Cherish the relationship you've built over time.

This should not be the "last" touchpoint in a perfect world as you want clients to stay with you for life if it serves them.

Nevertheless, you need to run this touchpoint to know if it makes sense to even offer them an option to continue to work with you.

If you understand the customer journey, you'll have a few raving fans, and this last touchpoint is a fantastic way to connect with them to understand:

- Why they love you so much?

- How you can double down on the things the fans love?

- How you can communicate the things your clients love about working with you in your marketing message.

For this to happen, you need to speak to your clients. You'll be surprised by how many business owners avoid this touchpoint and how much money they're losing every month because of that.

But there will be some clients you feel didn't love the service, so you need to find out more about unhappy customers and dedicate as much energy to this as you do to the ones that love you because:

- You will get real-world insights into how people feel about your business.

- You use their complaints to provide exceptional service.

You'll probably lose a few nights' sleep after the first few calls, but if you're willing to step up and act on this feedback, you'll make your business stand out in the marketplace.

You'll also find that this can be one of the best calls you'll ever have with clients. As a side effect, you'll get clients to upgrade and keep working with you, but the main focus of this call is to make them feel seen and heard again and use that feedback to keep innovating your offerings and your Fulfillment Funnel within those offerings.

Community

If you have a community for your clients to be a part of, you need to understand what to pay attention to to make it work long-term.

Clients who are confused or not bought in tend to check what others are doing and follow what they do.

A fantastic study by Dr. Nicholas Cristakis of Harvard Medical School followed 12,067 people for 32 years to understand some of their patterns and behaviors.

What they found was shocking. When someone became obese, the odds of that person's friends becoming obese as well tripled. Obesity was indeed contagious. This is also true when your community embodies frames like Persecutors and Victims. Beware of that.

When people embody the wrong behaviors, you want to avoid them. When they incorporate the right ones, promote them to get more buy-in and happier clients.

Celebrations

There is something that I feel is completely neglected in client experience. It is the opportunity to celebrate meaningful milestones and clients' achievements. We all love to be captured at our best, IG-worthy moment, a picture that tells a story.

You were brave, you conquered it, and you deserve recognition.

Do you remember this formula from the Expectation Management chapter?

$$\text{Expectations} = \text{Time} \times \text{Effort}$$

If you pay particular attention, when you think of effort, you think of hard work, which requires a lot of investment on your end as a client.

The same thing applies to time. There is an opportunity cost. Something that didn't get done because you decided to focus on the task at hand.

And at the end of the day, you expect to get better. This is why you started. Or at least that's what you think you want.

But what clients want is not only to get better, they want others to recognize that they're getting better. They want to enjoy a moment of recognition.

This will end up creating more buy-in from the client, which is good for everyone.

The challenging part in all of this is to find which moments should be celebrated. There are a couple of questions you can ask yourself:

- What's motivating for my clients?

- What would be worth celebrating within a short period of them starting the work with me?

- What's a hidden accomplishment that's worth celebrating?

Tough Love

All clients will have different tolerance levels for new challenges, so you must remember that gradually exposing them to challenges will help. They'll also need some tough love.

The tough love approach is probably slower than just spoon-feeding them and hand-holding them all the way, but it creates a great experience after a couple of weeks. If you want their Identity to grow while working with you, you want to increase their perception of your responsiveness.

This is the meaning of responsiveness:

- **Understanding**: feel seen

- **Validation**: feel respected for what I want

- **Caring**: I feel supported

A great example we use with our consulting clients are the questions from the Coaching Habit:

- What's on your mind? (focus on understanding, and make them feel seen)

- Tell me, what's the real challenge for you? (focuses on validation and makes them feel respected for what they want)

- How can I help? (focuses on caring and makes them feel

like you're supporting them in their needs)

Not only is this the perfect flow for effective communication, but this also builds massive reciprocity that can be considered social fuel.

Escalation

There will be moments of escalation even when you do a great job of implementing everything in this book. There will always be an outlier that gets your team spinning its wheels.

So you want to be ready for those conversations. If someone wants to drop out or if a client is very problematic, you can see these situations from two sides of the coin.

On the one hand, how can you manage and react to these situations? On the other hand, you want to understand how you can prevent these problems from happening beforehand.

Whenever you have a moment of escalation, the first step is to keep a Neutral Mindset and remove any attachments from this escalation to your self-worth. I know you care, and clients deserve the best, but you don't have complete control over what is happening at the end of the day.

And here is the time to look at the buy-in framework again:

- What looks like a people problem is often a situation

problem.

- What looks like laziness is often exhaustion.

- What looks like resistance is often a lack of clarity.

Understanding their frame of mind (drama triangle) and matching them with the right approach will give you a lot of leverage in this kind of discussion while also remembering and applying what you learned about the archetypes.

The approach for a Doer will be different from a Controller in an Escalation like this.

As an Ideal Customer Engineer, before having an interaction with a client that has escalated, reflect on these three areas:

- **The what happened conversation**: Sort out what happened.

    o *How do you see the situation?*

    o *Where does your story come from (information, past experiences, rules)?*

    o *What do you think you know about the other person's viewpoint?*

    o *What impact has this situation had on you?*

    o *What might their intentions have been?*

    o *What have you each contributed to the problem?*

- **The feelings conversation**: Understand your feelings.

  - *Explore your feelings and ask yourself, What emotions am I experiencing?*

- **The identity conversation**: Ground your identity.

  - *How does this situation threaten you or have the potential to shake up your sense of identity?*

  - *How do you see yourself (I'm the boss; I like competition; I'm loyal; I'm good at developing my people)?*

  - *What do you need to accept in order to be grounded?*

The strategy above will address any reactive response we need in a scenario of escalation. But if we want to make sure the majority of this book is applied as prevention, we need an excellent Tracking system to keep everything organized.

Tracking

Tracking is key to avoiding churn, drop-offs, short-duration contracts, and a team that's completely burnt out.

When we work with a consulting client, one of the first steps we focus on is their Tracking system. The tracking process gives us so much information that we can guarantee our business goals and a customer-centric offer.

The challenge comes from having too many data points; it's easy to get overwhelmed.

You will know what is working and what's not, detect patterns across your clients, understand which archetypes do better using your service, and know precise numbers for LTV, retention, and referrals. You will have Fulfillment Funnel KPIs and the most relevant metrics needed to fix and/or optimize your system.

Tracking is how you create leverage in your business, which is why we double down on that early on with clients.

Tracking will help with all the previous points discussed:

- Managing expectations.

- Tracking the relationship/buy-in.

- Keeping the Big Outcome top of mind, among other things.

This will help your delivery team to avoid dropouts before requests come, track refunds by archetype if any, and to be more proactive and less reactive.

You can do this effortlessly, and categorizing 2-4 KPIs as a traffic light system will give you more than enough information to focus on.

If you want to know more about it, feel free to contact us, and we can send you a walkthrough example.

Tracking can also help with one key ingredient of the High LTV offer equation: the time delay. When tracking your client progress, you can have an idea of where they are, which milestones they have accomplished so far, and which ones are approaching.

This is the ammunition you need in some of your crucial conversations with clients. You know that sometimes the Big Outcome they want can't happen from the get-go, but you know how you can plan and explain the milestones to get there.

When you know the milestones and understand that not all of your clients will be patient, you can frame this time as "preparation" time. While they achieve those "preparation" milestones, you can assure them they're on the right path.

Also, this keeps their Big Outcome top of mind; it's just the byproduct of hitting all the milestones planned for them. You keep the perceived likelihood of achievement high, which drives further action while reducing their perception of time delay.

A simple example is when a couple gets pregnant, they're not waiting nine months for the child. They're getting ready. The doctor's appointments, the crazy hours assembling the crib, and spending entire weekends thinking about which color to paint the bedroom. It's preparation, and it feels good after going through it.

Accelerating buy-in

You're probably tired of me using the expression: Buy-in. But at least you know how important it is!

I'm using repetition because it's one of the most important ideas in this book to guarantee a functional Fulfillment Funnel.

Knowing the importance of it, as soon as you have a Buy-in strategy, you focus on accelerating it even further. This will help with any remaining thirty-day churn you might still have and get it to zero, nada, niente.

Understanding the underlying psychology of it, you can double down on how to make it even more appealing for each archetype.

When you think about Controllers, they want to feel they can control their own journey. They're so used to it. But at the same time, you need to keep in mind that you're the expert and that you know more about the subject at hand than they do. If you can be a trusted advisor for a Controller, you will see them bought in.

On the other hand, Worriers are slightly different. You want them to feel 100% comfortable with the process in front of them and prevent any confusion so that they don't get stuck inside their own head in a debilitating thought process.

Our last archetype, the Followers, need to feel empowered to share how they feel along the journey and give them permission to not be okay. Remember that they tend to have complacency wired in them due to some sense of inferiority, and that being said, you want them to raise the standard with your support.

Rethinking the Client Journey

I thought long and hard about adding this part to the bonus section. This is one of the concepts we've become known for in the customer experience world, and I was unsure if it makes sense to share it with you without much more context, like when a client works with us.

But Ben challenged me to summarize it and give it to you as leverage, and then if you need help or more context, you can always reach out to us.

This is always the first type of work we do with clients so that we have both clarity and goals early in an engagement. This action plan and clarity will enable you to take advantage of the significant changes waiting for you in your business.

When going through this book, you'll have many ideas that will make you rethink your whole client journey and all the pieces involved:

- The interconnection between your acquisition and fulfillment funnels (bow-tie).

- Reviewing the offer's perceived value and all its ingredients, connecting them to different archetypes.

- Buy-in, escalation of commitment, and expectation management.

- Archetypes...

You name it. But instead of doing everything as I said before, try to tackle them one by one. How can you create an experience, leveraging psychology, so clients fully enjoy your offer?

Then you can go back to the drawing board to map out the critical touchpoints, which we call peaks and valleys. Those peaks and valleys are great moments for celebration and moments of insight, but they can also feel like inflection points.

Why did I leave this for the end? Because we need to have the foundation right to detect these moments before they happen and start to be more upstream-focused. This creates a real proactive customer experience.

This will give you another kind of edge: to understand how you can spot people who're doing okay and focus on making those clients great, the raving fans you want in your business. And you can finally position yourself as the trusted advisor who will keep working with them after their first purchase. Why wouldn't they continue?

But the experience must be memorable for that to happen, which is what this whole book is about: A True Relationship at Scale.

How your clients judge the experience will be based not on the number of days you've worked together but on some specific moments, the peaks, and the valleys.

This is what psychologists call the "duration neglect" effect. We tend to ignore how much time we spend in an experience, and we rate the experience based on two things:

- The highest high or lowest low (peak or valley).

- The ending.

Do you understand why I've spent the whole book talking about making the Peaks higher and the Valleys close to nonexistent?

So that you can also have a Raving Fan Formula inside your business.

Peaks and Valleys

We tend to confuse what it means to be excellent versus what it means to be remarkable. I'm sure you're awesome if you bought this book or if it was gifted to you. But that doesn't mean the experience you're providing for your clients is remarkable and memorable.

All the customer journeys you'll see will have a transitory movement between Peaks and Valleys. As a business owner or maybe an Ideal Customer Engineer, you want to elevate those Peaks and minimize the Valleys.

An excellent example shared in the Book *The Power of Moments* by the Heath Brothers is when you start a new sport.

Imagine you decide to learn Tennis, you go to the training facility, and the first day you show up, it completely sucks. But you won't quit. You show up a few days later with more confidence, and imagine what happens?

It sucks again. But over time, you see that it sucks less and less.

Then there is a day the trainer invites you to join an amateur championship to test your skills. The actual day has arrived.

Now it's time to show all of your development, and independent of the result, that day and that experience are memorable.

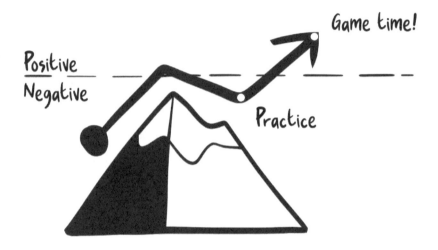

There is a severe lack of planning around the customer experience in the online and offline service industry. If you look at most services out there, they focus on having very few valleys, but you don't see any impressive peaks. You don't see celebrations or milestones that are worth remembering.

This experience looks bland, neutral, and not remarkable at all.

This is why some companies give awards to their clients to mark a milestone. They want to create a moment that's memorable, a moment of recognition.

You can do the same and create some great peaks and moments of joy when you engineer those celebrations.

The peaks along the customer journey should be celebrated. It helps with the following:

- Buy-in.

- Commitment.

- It motivates the emotional brain and keeps clients happy.

Let me share an example of how a company used peak architecture to make clients happy.

Pret A Manger gives employees a weekly budget with complimentary beverages and food items they can provide to clients randomly.

I haven't seen the same being done for online services. Giving your Ideal Customer Engineer a budget for them to delight a client every now and then will move many of those 4 clients (neutral state) into a 7 (Raving Fan).

So now equipped with what you know, I highly recommend you do an exercise called touchpoint mapping, where you map your client's journey. Things to plan ahead are:

1. What are the baseline touchpoints?

2. How can you plan moments to create buy-in?

3. What are the inflection points or valleys that need to be addressed?

4. How can you have triggers that will remind you to be preventative?

Start here, and you'll have a great baseline.

Now it's your turn to go back to your business and team and absolutely crush it. You can create a client-centric suite of offers that allow you to live a life of freedom, surrounded by Raving Fans and an Empowered Team. You are now ready to Ethically Scale!

VIII. RECOMMENDED READING

Our Top List

This is a short version of our recommended reading list. Some of these books are clearly highlighted and referred to in the Customer Success Manifesto book, while others are not. I can share with you that the list helped me shape my view on what we do today, and if you want to expand your knowledge, this is a solid baseline:

Thinking Fast and Slow by Danial Kahneman includes the concepts of the Slow and Fast brain reactions while also exploring Heuristics and Biases.

The Switch by Chip and Dan Heath explores the change model using stories and great examples, and it brings the buy-in framework to life.

Power of Moments by Chip and Dan Heath explores the science of creating memorable moments and experiences.

Upstream by Dan Heath explores the nature of thinking in reactive mode and how we can be more preventative with our approach to thinking upstream.

Nudge by Richard Thaler explores how small tweaks in the environment and how we approach people can dramatically change their behavior.

The Happiness Hypothesis by Jonathan Haidt introduces the concept we use for the Emotional Brain and Logical Brain through the lens of an Elephant and a Rider.

The Chimp Paradox by Professor Steve Peters brings to life a similar concept to the one explored in the Happiness Hypothesis, but instead of an Elephant and a Rider, he used the Chimp, The Human, and the Computer.

Predictably Irrational by Dan Ariely explains how we make some decisions we do in our life.

Adam Grant, in his book, *Think Again,* challenged me to look back at where we stand regarding our beliefs and be more open to challenge and Think Again.

The Happiness Advantage by Shawn Anchor talks about great principles for change while feeling good about yourself, including the Hopelessness concept described in the Customer Success Manifesto.

George Leonard's book, *Mastery: The Keys to Success and Long-Term Fulfillment,* inspired me to look at different archetypes from an inner fulfillment standpoint in order to provide our clients with what they really want from life.

The Coaching Habit by Michael Bungay Stanier introduced me to a very simple framework to ask great questions to clients without creating codependency or falling prey to the Drama Triangle.

What Customers Crave by Nicholas Webb is a great book that touches on several ideas on what we should be looking for regarding the customer experience.

Effortless Experience by Matthew Dixon is a great book that covers studies and groundbreaking summaries around what clients want regarding support and loyalty.

The Diffusion of Innovations is a great book that covers multiple examples and ideas on how our ideas spread through the marketplace.

Alex Hormozi's $100M Offers book introduced the perceived value concept around offers that we used extensively in this Customer Success Manifesto book.

Building a Storybrand by Donald Miller is a fantastic book with probably one of the best interpretations of how you should see your role as a Customer Guide.

Alchemy by Rory Sutherland has too many nuggets to describe in one single sentence; he's my favorite Marketer in the whole world while also being Vice Chairmen of the Ogilvy Foundation.

Richard Koch, in his book *The Star Principle*, explores the ideas of a Star business, the Cash Cow Concepts, and introduced me to the story of Belgo shared in this book.

Made in United States
Troutdale, OR
01/03/2025

27570567R00176